THURGOOD MARSHALL

THURGOOD MARSHALL

A Biography

Glenn L. Starks and F. Erik Brooks

GREENWOOD BIOGRAPHIES

 GREENWOOD

AN IMPRINT OF ABC-CLIO, LLC
Santa Barbara, California • Denver, Colorado • Oxford, England

Library of Congress Cataloging-in-Publication Data

Starks, Glenn L., 1966–
 Thurgood Marshall : a biography / Glenn L. Starks, F. Erik Brooks.
 p. cm. — (Greenwood biographies)
 Includes index.
 ISBN 978-0-313-34916-4 (hardback) — ISBN 978-0-313-34917-1
(ebook) 1. Marshall, Thurgood, 1908–1993. 2. United States. Supreme
Court—Biography. 3. African American judges—Biography. 4. Judges—
United States—Biography. I. Brooks, F. Erik. II. Title.
 KF8745.M34S73 2012
 347.73'2634—dc23
 [B] 2011051894

ISBN: 978-0-313-34916-4
EISBN: 978-0-313-34917-1

16 15 14 13 12 1 2 3 4 5

This book is also available on the World Wide Web as an eBook.
Visit www.abc-clio.com for details.

Greenwood
An Imprint of ABC-CLIO, LLC

ABC-CLIO, LLC
130 Cremona Drive, P.O. Box 1911
Santa Barbara, California 93116-1911

This book is printed on acid-free paper ∞

Manufactured in the United States of America

CONTENTS

CONTENTS

SERIES FOREWORD

In response to school and library needs, ABC-CLIO publishes this distinguished series of full-length biographies specifically for student use. Prepared by field experts and professionals, these engaging biographies are tailored for students who need challenging yet accessible biographies. Ideal for school assignments and student research, the length, format, and subject areas are designed to meet educators' requirements and students' interests.

ABC-CLIO offers an extensive selection of biographies spanning all curriculum-related subject areas including social studies, the sciences, literature and the arts, history and politics, and popular culture, covering public figures and famous personalities from all time periods and backgrounds, both historic and contemporary, who have made an impact on American and/or world culture. The subjects of these biographies were chosen based on comprehensive feedback from librarians and educators. Consideration was given to both curriculum relevance and inherent interest. Readers will find a wide array of subject choices from fascinating entertainers like Miley Cyrus and Lady Gaga to inspiring leaders like John F. Kennedy and Nelson Mandela, from the greatest athletes of our time like Michael Jordan and Lance Armstrong

to the most amazing success stories of our day like J.K. Rowling and Oprah.

While the emphasis is on fact, not glorification, the books are meant to be fun to read. Each volume provides in-depth information about the subject's life from birth through childhood, the teen years, and adulthood. A thorough account relates family background and education, traces personal and professional influences, and explores struggles, accomplishments, and contributions. A timeline highlights the most significant life events against an historical perspective. Bibliographies supplement the reference value of each volume.

INTRODUCTION

Thurgood Marshall remains one of the most prolific and influential figures in American legal and civil rights history. His success in winning landmark Supreme Court cases ending racial segregation was the foundation of African Americans gaining equal rights in education, politically and socially. He was also a champion for women's rights, the poor, the mentally ill, and ensuring those convicted of crimes were afforded due process under the law. Because of his skills and experience as a lawyer, he gained further success in public service. From being appointed a Circuit Court Judge and then the first African American U. S. solicitor general, he then became the first African American appointed to the Supreme Court of the United States. His indelible influence on law is evidenced by the countless cases that have been tried since his retirement from the Supreme Court that are based on precedents he either argued himself as a lawyer or ruled on as a judge. An editorial in the *Washington Afro-American* after Thurgood's death describes the impact of his accomplishments: "We make movies about Malcolm X, we get a holiday to honor Dr. Martin Luther King, but every day we live with the legacy of Justice Thurgood Marshall."

While he is celebrated as one of the most important and influential African American figures in history, Thurgood spent his life not only championing causes that benefited African Americans but also all Americans. A quote by Duke University Professor John Hope Franklin in *Ebony* magazine appropriately speaks to Thurgood's legacy:

> If you study the history of Marshall's career, the history of his rulings on the Supreme Court, even his dissents, you will understand that when he speaks, he is not speaking just for black Americans but for Americans of all times. He reminds us constantly of the great promise this country has made of equality, and he reminds us that it has not been fulfilled. Through his life he has been a great watchdog, insisting that this nation live up to the Constitution. (*Ebony*, 1990, p. 68)

Beyond being a brilliant lawyer, Thurgood Marshall is remembered as a storyteller, for his humor, and for his ability to turn the lessons of his own life into a commitment to make life better for everyone.

TIMELINE: EVENTS IN THE LIFE OF THURGOOD MARSHALL

July 2, 1908 Thoroughgood (Thurgood) Marshall is born in Baltimore, Maryland.

1909 The National Association for the Advancement of Colored People (NAACP) founded.

1921 Enrolls at the Colored High and Training School.

1923 Colored High and Training School is renamed Frederick Douglass High School.

1925 Enrolls at Lincoln University in Chester County, Pennsylvania.

1927 Becomes a member of Alpha Phi Alpha Fraternity, Inc., which was founded in 1906.

1929 Marries Vivian "Buster" Burey.

1930 Graduates cum laude from Lincoln University.

1930 Is denied admission to the University of Maryland School of Law because of his race. Instead, he enrolls at the Howard University Law School where he meets mentor Charles Hamilton Houston.

1933 Graduates first in his class (magna cum laude) from Howard University Law School and opens a private law practice in Baltimore.

1934 Begins to work for the Baltimore branch of the NAACP.

1936 With mentor and friend Charles Hamilton Houston, wins first major civil rights case, *Murray v. Pearson*, 182 A. 590 (Md. 1936), desegregating the University of Maryland School of Law.

1936 Becomes assistant special counsel for the NAACP in New York.

1938 With the assistance of Thurgood, Charles Hamilton Houston becomes the first African American to argue and win a case before the United States Supreme Court, *Missouri ex rel. Gaines v. Canada*, 305 U.S. 337 (1938).

1940–1961 Serves as legal director of the NAACP. He wins 29 out of the 32 Supreme Court cases he argues during this time.

1940 Wins the first of his Supreme Court victories, *Chambers v. Florida*, 309 U.S. 227 (1940), in which police unlawfully used pressure to obtain a criminal confession.

1943 Wins case for integration of schools in Hillburn, New York.

1944 Successfully argues *Smith v. Allwright*, 321 U.S. 649 (1944) before the Supreme Court, overthrowing the Democratic Party's practice of only allowing whites to vote in Southern primary elections.

1946 Wins the NAACP Spingarn Medal for outstanding achievements as a lawyer.

1946 Wins *Irene Morgan v. Commonwealth of Virginia*, 328 U.S. 373 (1946), in which the Supreme Court desegregates seating on interstate buses.

1947 Wins *Patton v. Mississippi*, 332 U.S. 463 (1947), with the Supreme Court ruling against strategies that exclude African Americans from serving on criminal juries.

1948 Wins *Shelley v. Kraemer*, 334 U.S. 1 (1948), in which Supreme Court strikes down the legality of racially restrictive covenants prohibiting the sale of real property to African Americans.

1948 Wins *Sipuel v. Board of Regents of University of Oklahoma*, 332 U.S. 631 (1948), in which the Supreme Court ruled Oklahoma could not bar African American students from its all-white law school.

1950 Wins *McLaurin v. Oklahoma State Regents*, 339 U.S. 637 (1950), in which the Supreme Court reversed a lower court decision supporting segregated graduate and professional schools in Oklahoma.

1950 Wins Supreme Court victories in two graduate school integration cases, *Sweatt v. Painter*, 339 U.S. 629 (1950) and *McLaurin v. Oklahoma State Regents*, 339 U.S. 637 (1950).

1950 Charles Hamilton Houston dies at the age of 55.

1951 Visits South Korea and Japan at the request of President Harry S. Truman to investigate charges of racism in the United States armed forces.

1954 Wins *Brown v. Board of Education of Topeka*, 347 U.S. 483 (1954) before the Supreme Court, the landmark lawsuit that ends the legal segregation of public schools in the United States.

February 1955 Wife Vivian "Buster" Marshall dies.

December 1955 Marries Cecilia A. Suyat. Their marriage produces Thurgood's two sons, Thurgood Marshall Jr. and John William Marshall.

1956 Wins *Browder v. Gayle*, 352 U.S. 903 (1956), in which the Supreme Court ends the practice of segregation on buses. This case ends the Montgomery Bus Boycott being led by Dr. Martin Luther King Jr.

1957 Founds and becomes the first president-director counsel of the NAACP Legal Defense and Educational Fund, Inc., a nonprofit law firm separate and independent of the NAACP.

1960 Travels to Kenya to assist in the development of that country's new constitution as it prepares to become independent of Great Britain.

1961 Defends civil rights demonstrators, winning Supreme Court victory in *Garner v. Louisiana*, 368 U.S. 157 (1961).

1961 Nominated and appointed to the U.S. Court of Appeals, 2nd Circuit by President John F. Kennedy. Makes 112 rulings, all of them later upheld by the Supreme Court.

1963 The Republic of Kenya gains independence from Great Britain.

1965 Appointed as the first African American United States Solicitor General by President Lyndon Johnson. Wins 14 of the 19 cases he argues on behalf of the government through 1967.

1967 Becomes first African American appointed to the U.S. Supreme Court.

1970 Third College in La Jolla, California is founded and later renamed Thurgood Marshall College in 1993 by the University of California, San Diego.

1976 The Texas Southern University School of Law is renamed in his honor.

1978 Makes an adamant dissenting opinion in *Regents of the University of California v. Bakke*, 438 U.S. 265 (1978), in which the Supreme Court ruled against affirmative action being used in higher education admissions decisions.

1980 The University of Maryland Law School Library is named in his honor.

1987 The Thurgood Marshall College Fund established.

1991 Retires from the Supreme Court.

1992 The Thurgood Marshall Award is established in his honor by the American Bar Association.

1992 The Thurgood Marshall Federal Judiciary Building is completed in Washington, DC.

1992 Receives the Liberty Medal recognizing his long history of protecting individual rights under the Constitution.

1993 Dies at age 84 in Bethesda, Maryland. He is buried in Arlington National Cemetery.

1993 Receives Presidential Medal of Freedom, posthumously, from President Bill Clinton.

1993 The University of Maryland renames law school library to the Thurgood Marshall Law Library.

2005 The Baltimore-Washington International Airport is re-
 named the Baltimore-Washington International Thur-
 good Marshall Airport.
2010 Laurence Fishburne stars in the critically acclaimed one-
 man play, *Thurgood*.
2010 May 17 is declared as Thurgood Marshall Day in the state
 of New York annually.
2010 Elena Kagan, a former Supreme Court law clerk for
 Thurgood, is confirmed as an Associate Justice on the
 Supreme Court.

Chapter 1

EARLY LIFE

Thurgood Marshall was born "Thoroughgood Marshall" on July 2, 1908, in west Baltimore, Maryland. He was originally called both Thorneygood and Thoroughgood after his paternal grandfather, Thorney Good Marshall (September 1849–January 10, 1915), who changed his name after he joined the Union Army during the Civil War. His grandfather couldn't decide which name he wanted, so he kept them both and even eventually received two retirement checks from the army. Thurgood was the second and youngest of the two sons of William Canfield Marshall (March 25, 1882–February 25, 1948) and his wife Norma Arica Williams Marshall (August 13, 1885–August 1961), who were married on April 17, 1905.

Norma was named after Bellini's opera, which her father heard in the South American seaport of Arica. Her father, Isaiah Williams (January 7, 1838–March 21, 1894), had served in the U.S. Navy and he and his wife, Mary Fossett (April 1849–July 21, 1926), gave all of their six children unusual names. Norma's sister Denmedia was named for a grocery store their father owned on Denmead Street in Baltimore. One of their brothers was named Fearless Mentor because he stared fearlessly into his father's eyes when he was born. The other siblings

were named Avonia, Avon, and Ravine. Norma became an elementary school teacher after graduating from Coppin State University in Baltimore in 1905. She later became one of the first African Americans to graduate from Columbia Teacher's College in New York City. Her mother, Mary Fossett Williams, had also been a teacher at a private black academy in Baltimore and her sister, Avonia, was one of the first black teachers in a black public school. Norma's family so valued education that her mother insisted she finish college when William and Norma announced their plans to marry. She also insisted William pay for Norma's education. After marrying, she soon gave birth to their eldest son, William Aubrey (who was called Aubrey) in 1906 and put her teaching career on hold to care for him.

Thurgood's father William worked as a railroad porter for the Baltimore and Ohio Railroad, and as head steward at the Gibson Island Club, a prestigious all-white club on Chesapeake Bay in Baltimore that blacks and Jews were not allowed to join. He was the eldest boy of his six siblings—Mary, Thoroughgood, Anne, Cyrus, Thomas, and Marg Marshall. His mother Annie E. Robinson (June 1857–February 6, 1948) married his father in December 1879. One of William's achievements was becoming the first African American in the 20th century to serve on a grand jury in Baltimore.

While Thurgood grew up in a comfortable middle-class family (both of his grandparents owned large grocery stores in Baltimore), his maternal great-grandfather was a slave who was born in Zaire, which is today called the Democratic Republic of the Congo. Thurgood said his great-grandfather became a slave after "a rich man from Maryland went to the Congo on a hunting expedition" and his great-grandfather, then just a boy, followed the man to his boat. The man thought he was getting a slave for free and brought him back to the United States with him. As the boy grew older as a slave, he became what Thurgood described "one mean man." The rich man told the boy, "you're too ornery to keep and too ornery to sell to a white" so he would set him free "if you'll get out of the town and country and state." Thurgood's great-grandfather replied, "I ain't going nowhere." He settled down a few miles from his master's home and was never bothered by the slave owner again (Tushnet, 1994, p. 8).

When Thurgood was two years old, his family moved to Harlem, New York and near his mother's sister, Denmedia. Denmedia told William he could get steady work with her husband, Clarence, as a waiter, which gave William the opportunity to get a better job with the New York Central Railroad. It was during this time that Norma attended Columbia University's Teachers College. When he was very young, Thurgood, whose nickname was Goody, learned to cry to get what he wanted. After being treated for a hernia, he overheard the doctor tell his mother not to let him cry. His mother soon figured out he was using crying as a form of manipulation and punished him. He didn't do it again. He gained the nickname Goody because he often brought stray animals and even people to the family's apartment and pleaded with his mother to feed them.

The Marshall family returned to Baltimore in 1914 to care for the children's grandmother after she broke her leg. They lived with Norma's brother, Fearless Mentor Williams, and his wife, Flo. Their neighborhood was predominantly black, but their next door neighbors were a white Jewish family. The neighborhood also consisted of Russian, Italian, and German immigrants. Fearless and Flo had no children of their own, so spent a lot of time with Thurgood and Aubrey. Thurgood's father was often gone for days when working on the railroad, but "Uncle Fee," as the boys called Fearless, was home every afternoon and night. During the day, Fearless worked as a personal attendant to the white president of the B&O Railroad and so was on first-name basis with the Baltimore's white business leaders and politicians. Fearless went to work each day wearing a suit and bow-ties, and was a positive influence for Thurgood and his brother.

Thurgood began school at the age of six and attended Number 103, considered to be the best "colored" elementary school in Baltimore. Although he was raised in a stable middle-class home, he hung out in the "back alleys where the roughnecks and the tough kids hung out." Thurgood later recalled, "When it was time for dinner, my mother used to go to the front door and call my older brother. Then she'd go to the back door and call me" (Goldman and Gallen, 1992, p. 24). Because her son often got in trouble, Norma made Thurgood attend the schools where she was teaching. He was a very strong-willed child. While in the second

grade and six years old, Thoroughgood shortened his name to Thurgood because he disliked the spelling of his unusual long name and other children teased him about his nickname. He had his mother to officially change his name on his birth certificate. In school, he was often loud and caused disturbances during class. He teased other students and some of his teachers sat him on the front row in the classroom to keep an eye on him. Starting in grade school, his punishment for misbehaving was to be sent to the basement to learn sections of the Constitution which he had to recite before returning to class. He was able to recite the Constitution from memory by the time he graduated high school at age 16.

Thurgood's behavior in school was not unlike that of his father when he was growing up. William never graduated high school because he was a trouble-making student who did not fear his teachers or school administrators. During an interview, Thurgood stated that "The high school notified my grandfather that my father had misbehaved. My grandfather went to the high school, took my father into the hall, and whipped him in the presence of all the other students. Pop was so embarrassed that he never went back to school" (Crowe, 2008, p. 38). After quitting school, William took odd jobs before working in his family's grocery store. It was from there that he learned the importance of hard work and the value of money.

Thurgood learned about segregation at an early age. When he was older, he often said he was born "way up South in Baltimore" because segregation there in his youth was just as harsh as anywhere in the Deep South. In later life, Thurgood commented on a study done by the Urban League in 1930 that revealed the segregation in Baltimore was more rigid than any other city in the country, including Jackson, Mississippi. He would hear his parents discussing racial crimes and lynchings. Democrats took control of the city in 1899 with a campaign slogan "This Is a White Man's City." City council members fought over the issue of wealthy blacks moving into predominantly white neighborhoods. Democrats not only sought to forbid blacks from desegregating these areas, but also whites from moving into predominantly black areas. Democrats attempted to take away the right for blacks to vote in 1904, but were defeated by Republicans and African American citizens. The city was segregated and racial tension was high to the point that there were numerous instances of black women being sexu-

ally accosted by white men. Most local store owners were Jewish, and blacks were not allowed in many stores. While in downtown Baltimore on a Saturday, Thurgood had to use the bathroom but couldn't because blacks were not allowed to use the public restrooms. He ran home and later recalled that he almost made it into his house, but ended up ruining the front doorsteps.

During an interview in 1977, Thurgood stated, "We used to have fight with the white kids, just on general principles. There was a white Catholic elementary school two blocks from Division Street, and for some reason, we didn't get along very well. They were practically all Italians, and we used to have periodic fights—not too bad. Maybe a rock here and there. It was fists, and eventually (the white school) let them out fifteen minutes before we got out, so that they could get home" (Smith and Ellis, 2011). Thurgood explained in another interview that he never grew up hating white people because there were some that touched his life and he considered very good people. For example, in high school he worked for a Jewish man named Mortimer Schoen as a delivery boy. Thurgood recalled an afternoon he was delivering hats from Schoen's elite dress shop. Thurgood took the trolley car, boarded ahead of a white woman, and was grabbed and pulled back by a white man who said "Nigger, don't you push in front of white people." The two got into a fight and Thurgood was arrested. At the police station, Schoen arrived and offered to bail Thurgood out. When Schoen also got his lawyer, Thurgood was released. Schoen promised to pay for Thurgood and his brother to go to college but died before either of them was old enough to go.

In another incident, a 16-year-old Thurgood was applying for a job as a porter on the railroad. He was interviewed by a white conductor who told him "Ok boy, you can have the job. Here's your uniform put it on." Thurgood returned and told the conductor the pants were too short. In response, the conductor told him, "Boy, it's easier to get another nigger than another pair of pants. You want the job you wear the pants" (Smith and Ellis, 2011). Thurgood took the job because he was saving money for college. However, he did not want another generation to live in a society where someone could freely make such harsh statements to another human being.

Thurgood's parents taught him and his brother racial pride and self-esteem. Although he was very light complexioned with blond hair and

blue eyes and could have passed for white as other blacks of his complexion did at the time, William never did because he was proud of his race. He used phrases such as "That's right black of you" to praise his sons and teach them racial pride. When he criticized them, he would use such phrases as "That's the white man in the wood pile." He told his sons that "If anyone calls you nigger, you not only got my permission to fight him—you got my orders to fight him" (Smith and Ellis, 2011). As an adult Thurgood recalled, "My dad and my mother both used to tell us that we had what everybody else had. And the fact that you happened to be a different color didn't mean anything. My dad would say that my mother was the prettiest brown-skinned woman in the world. And my mother would say, 'Brown-skinned? No, I'm the prettiest woman in the world'" (Crowe, 2008, p. 54). Thurgood's parents encouraged him to become a professional when he grew up. His grandmother taught him how to cook, explaining "Your mother and father want you to be a dentist or a doctor, something like that. And I hope you make it. But just in case you don't, I'm going to teach you how to cook. And you know why? You've never seen an unemployed black cook" (Williams, 1998, p. 27).

Thurgood's father taught his son to appreciate the rule of law and the U.S. Constitution. Since the family lived close to a police station, his father also took him there to watch people being questioned and to watch court trials. His parents taught him and his brother to argue and prove every statement they made during debates at the dinner table. These debates would include the parents challenging their children on key points. Thurgood later said that his father "never told me to become a lawyer, he turned me into one" (United States Court, 2011). Thurgood's father also made him read the newspaper every day.

Thurgood began attending the all-black Colored High and Training School in 1921 as a ninth grade freshman. At the same time, his mother Norma went back to school and enrolled at Morgan College to renew her teaching license. Thurgood's high school didn't have a library, a cafeteria, or a gym. The school was so overcrowded that students were divided into half-day sessions so that all the students could attend. Students were also divided into different classes based upon test scores they took on entry exams as freshman. Thurgood was placed in the class with the best students, served on the student council, and led the

debate team. He took classes such as trigonometry, physics, Latin, history, machine work, and wood training. Because he was tall and lanky, his classmates nicknamed him Legs. He was also very popular, played football, and dated lots of girls. Thurgood graduated from the "Colored High School," as it was called (but renamed Frederick Douglas High School in 1923), in 1925. He graduated a year early with a B average, in the top third of his class, and with a certificate for good attendance. His achievements were surprising given he didn't take school very seriously and didn't like to study.

Both Thurgood and his brother William Aubrey enrolled at the then all-male Lincoln University in Chester County, Pennsylvania, the oldest historically black college or university in the United States. The college was called the Black Princeton because it was founded by the same Presbyterians who ran Princeton University. Many of the all-white staff members at Lincoln were graduates of Princeton. Lincoln was originally named Ashmun Institute when it was founded in 1854 but its name was changed to Lincoln University in 1866 after the assassination of President Abraham Lincoln.

Aubrey, who was a senior when Thurgood enrolled as a freshman, was interested in medicine and eventually became a chest surgeon. Norma wanted Thurgood to become a dentist so he initially enrolled as a pre-medical student. His classmates included such notable future leaders as poet and author Langston Hughes, future Ghana President Kwame Nkrumah, and bandleader and musician Cab Calloway. Thurgood was very impressed by his classmates. He described Hughes as "one of the greatest people I've ever known. He knew everything there was to be known. He'd been around the world twice when he was twenty-one on tramp steamers. He studied and he just self studied and then he went to Lincoln. He was a great guy. I liked him" (Williams, 1998).

Thurgood brought the same lax attitude he had toward studying in high school with him to college, but worked several jobs to pay for his tuition. He was 17 when he enrolled at Lincoln and eager to have fun. During his first two years, he played cards, loved cowboy movies, read comic books, and formed the Weekend Club whose members only stayed on campus during the weekend if there was a football game. Otherwise, they took the train into Philadelphia where blacks could go to theaters, restaurants, and nightclubs. During his second year,

he became a member of Alpha Phi Alpha Fraternity, Inc., which was founded in 1906 at Cornell University as the nation's first black fraternity. Thurgood seldom studied but did become a star on the debating team. Langston Hughes became friends with Thurgood and got him interested in race issues. Thurgood read W.E.B. Du Bois's *The Souls of Black Folk* and his editorials in the National Association for the Advancement of Colored People's (NAACP) magazine *The Crisis*. This interest would influence Thurgood throughout his later life.

Beginning in Thurgood's sophomore year at Lincoln, he made several life changing decisions. He met Vivian "Buster" Burey and married her on September 4, 1929 during the start of his junior year. Vivian was a student at the University of Pennsylvania and the two met during a weekend trip Thurgood took to Philadelphia. Vivian influenced Thurgood to become a more serious student. He had previously been suspended twice for fraternity pranks and hazing fraternity pledges. He lost his interest in dentistry, mainly because of frequent arguments with a biology professor who was part of the university's all-white faculty. He became a star debater in the Forensic Society in his senior year. Thurgood graduated from Lincoln in June 1930 with honors (cum laude) and received a B.A. degree in Humanities, with a major in American literature and philosophy.

After graduating from Lincoln, Thurgood wanted to return to Baltimore and attend the University of Maryland School of Law. The school was near his parents' home and offered in-state tuition. To save money for school, he worked as an insurance agent and waited tables at the Gibson Island Club. Vivian worked as a secretary. Thurgood didn't apply to the University of Maryland because he knew he would not be admitted because of the university's segregative all-white enrollment policy. Instead, he then decided to attend the historically black Howard University School of Law. His mother so believed in her son that she pawned her engagement rings and wedding rings to pay for Thurgood's entry fees to Howard. Thurgood and his wife lived with his parents to save money, so he commuted to Washington, D.C. every day by train after getting up at five every morning and returned home around eight at night. He would eat dinner and then study until midnight. After his first year, he lost 40 pounds from this grueling pace. He soon got a job as an assistant in the Howard University law

library because he became a top student in his first year. As a student librarian, he spent most of his time reading law books. Thurgood still remained deeply troubled by the policy followed by the University of Maryland. This would be one of the impetuses for his endeavors later in his life.

At Howard, Thurgood once said that he really studied there for the first time in his life. He met and was immediately influenced by the law school's dynamic new dean, Charles Hamilton Houston (September 3, 1895–April 22, 1950). Houston transformed Howard's law school into a school to train leaders to fight discrimination. Thurgood described Houston as "hell bent on establishing a cadre of Negro lawyers, dedicated to fighting for equal rights . . . to do something for Negroes as such, and . . . to raise the image of the Negro Lawyers" (Tushnet, 1994, p. 6). Houston criticized older African American lawyers as only seeking to exploit their clients for their own personal interests. He felt young lawyers, on the other hand, had a conception of their privilege and responsibility. They would, therefore, represent their clients to make life better for their race and to ensure the law was used as a vehicle to improve society for everyone.

Houston was born in Washington, D.C. in 1895. He graduated valedictorian and Phi Beta Kappa from Amherst College in 1915 when he was 19 years old and then joined the U.S. Army, serving in a segregated unit during World War I. He served as a First Lieutenant in the infantry and later wrote, "The hate and scorn showered on us Negro officers by our fellow Americans convinced me that there was no sense in my dying for a world ruled by them. I made up my mind that if I got through this war I would study law and use my time fighting for men who could not strike back" (Armstead, 2009, p. 97). After the war, he began studying law at Harvard University in 1919 and became the first African American editor of the prestigious Harvard Law Review in 1922. He earned a Ph.D. in juridical science from Harvard in 1923 and then a doctor of civil law degree from the University of Madrid in Spain. Houston was a protégé of Harvard professor Felix Frankfurter, who later became a Supreme Court Justice. To honor the lifetime achievements of Houston, in 2005 Professor Charles J. Ogletree Jr. established the Charles Hamilton Houston Institute for Race and Justice (CHHIRJ) at Harvard Law School.

Houston joined Howard's law school faculty in 1924 after moving back to Washington, D.C. to practice law with his father. He became dean by 1930. Before he implemented his plan to turn the Howard Law School into the "West Point of Negro leadership," the school only offered courses at night to working students and most instructors were practicing attorneys who taught as a secondary job. The school was known as the dummy's retreat because it admitted students who were not intelligent enough to gain admission to better law schools. Upon becoming dean, Houston redesigned the curriculum, ended the night division, and secured accreditation from the Association of American Law Schools. He brought lawyers and scholars from Harvard to give lectures and built a new law library. Houston designed tactics to push the Howard law students to excel. During their first year, he would tell them to look at the men on their right and left because by the next year two of them would not be there. This statement proved to be true. Out of the 30 students that began in Thurgood's class, only 6 eventually graduated. Houston also stated that it never gave him pleasure to fail an average student, but he did enjoy failing the brightest students. He instituted the "cutback" program in which a professor could take five points from a student's grade at their discretion. This meant students had to excel even more to maintain a high grade. He positively pushed the students by telling them they had to be better than white lawyers because they would never be treated as equals. Therefore, they had to overcome being treated unequally because of their race by being exceptional lawyers.

Houston instilled in Thurgood and other students the importance of applying the principles of the Constitution when practicing law to fight discrimination, and that they should all strive to be social engineers of change. Houston once said that "A lawyer's either a social engineer or he's a parasite on society" (Bureau of International Information Program, 2008, p. 26). Thurgood and other students would sit with Houston, William H. Hastie, Andrew Ransom, and others and discuss ways to attack segregation. They would debate, research and study strategies to dismantle it. Houston believed the "separate but equal" doctrine that was established by the Supreme Court in their ruling in *Plessy v. Ferguson*, 163 U.S. 537 (1896) should be overturned. In this case, the Supreme Court ruled that state laws requiring racial

segregation were constitutional as long as blacks and whites were provided equal facilities.

Thurgood graduated first in his class, magna cum laude, from Howard in 1933. The dean of Harvard Law School, Roscoe Pound, offered him a one-year scholarship toward an SJD degree in constitutional law. The scholarship would have covered his tuition and housing for Thurgood and his family. However, Thurgood turned it down because he immediately wanted to practice law. After passing the Maryland Bar exam, he opened a modest solitary law practice in the Baltimore area and represented clients in civil and criminal cases. It was a difficult economic time to open a practice. The city was suffering from the Great Depression and most members of the African American community were domestic servants or working common labor jobs. The city government didn't have many relief programs and was particularly disinterested in assisting the African American community.

Thurgood got assistance from Warner McGuinn, one of the first African Americans to graduate from Yale Law School. McGuinn allowed Thurgood to run his practice in an office next to his own and

Thurgood Marshall, attorney for the NAACP, 1957. (Library of Congress.)

often helped Thurgood from making legal mistakes. His practice made so little money that he took a job at a city health clinic as a file clerk two nights a week and on Saturdays. During his first year, Thurgood's practice lost $3,500 because he couldn't get enough cases. His mother visited his small office decorated with second-hand furniture. She insisted his office needed a rug. Because Thurgood couldn't afford one, his mother went back to her house and brought the rug from her living room floor to his office. Thurgood's cases often involved representing women who wanted to get divorces, settling tenant–landlord disputes, and representing misdemeanor offenders, and small claims cases. However, he soon secured more substantial clients including a large laundry, the association of African American funeral directors, and Carl Murphy, the publisher of the Baltimore *Afro-American*.

While he couldn't afford it, Thurgood began to fight segregation in the city. He represented the local NAACP in negotiating with white store owners who sold to blacks but would not hire them. He also joined John L. Lewis in his efforts to unionize black and white steelworkers. Lewis served as president of the United Mine Workers of America from 1920 until 1960 and led to the founding of the Congress of Industrial Organizations (CIO). The CIO established the United Steel Workers of America which unionized millions of industrial workers.

Chapter 2

LAWYER FOR THE NAACP

Thurgood was 25 years old when he opened his private law practice in Baltimore in 1933. At first his cases were modest, with him representing local residents in civil and criminal cases. However, he was deeply involved in the Baltimore branch of the NAACP. He and civic leader Lillie Jackson worked to reinvigorate the branch because it had been failing since the late 1920s. Thurgood spoke at branch meetings, centering his topic to members on Charles Hamilton Houston's lessons that the law could be used to change society. This caused him to take on even more clients who were unable to pay him. He soon realized he could not continue to operate a practice for free, but he wanted to expand his work with the NAACP in order to change the laws. The primary policy he wanted to change was segregation in education because of his prior inability to get into the University of Maryland's law school.

In the late 1920s, the NAACP developed a relationship with the American Fund for Public Service. This was an organization also known as the Garland Fund, which received its money from Charles Garland. Garland set up the fund while attending Harvard College in 1922 with $800,000 from his inheritance because he felt the money came

from exploitation of the working class. He established the foundation to fund radical racial reform. Roger Baldwin ran the Garland Fund, as well directing the American Civil Liberties Union (ACLU). The fund gave the NAACP a grant of $100,000 to study the legal status of African Americans. The NAACP hired Nathan Margold, a former assistant U.S. attorney for the Southern District of New York, and he focused his report on discrimination in public schools. He completed his 218-page legal-sized paper report in 1931, and it documented the extreme underfunding of black segregated schools compared to white schools by state. He advised the NAACP to challenge the constitutional validity of underfunded black schools on the grounds that it violated the Equal Protection Clause of the Fourteenth Amendment.

Thurgood wrote a letter to Conrad Pearson, a 1932 Howard University graduate, asking for the papers from a lawsuit Pearson had filed on behalf of Thomas R. Hocutt. Hocutt was denied admission to the University of North Carolina pharmacy school. His lawsuit (*Hocutt v. Wilson* (N.C. Super. Ct. 1933)) failed because the president of the black school Hocutt had attended, President James Shepard of the North Carolina State College for Negroes, refused to provide him with an official transcript and copies of recommendation letters. Shepard felt challenging segregation would hurt the operation of his college. Thurgood wanted to use the notes from the lawsuit to prepare a case against the University of Maryland.

By this time, Houston was serving as special counsel for the NAACP. He accepted this position in 1934. In addition to Thurgood, Houston surrounded himself with other young lawyers who were mostly graduates of Howard Law School. These included James Nabrit Jr., Spottswood William Robinson III, Aloyisus Leon Higginbotham Jr., Robert Lee Carter, William Henry Hastie Jr., George Edward Chalmer Hayes, Jack Greenberg, and Oliver White Hill Sr. It is particularly noteworthy that all these men became active in civil rights and achieved high levels of prominence in later life. Nabrit served as the president of Howard University from 1960 until 1965, and then as deputy U.S. ambassador to the United Nations. Robinson became the first African American appointed to the U.S. Court of Appeals for the District of Columbia Circuit Court in 1966 under President Lyndon Johnson, and then the first African American chief judge of the District of Columbia Circuit

Court. Higginbotham became the seventh African American Article III judge appointed in the United States and the first African American judge on the U.S. District Court for the Eastern District of Pennsylvania. He received the Presidential Medal of Freedom from President Bill Clinton in 1995. Carter was appointed as a judge of the U.S. District Court for the Southern District of New York in 1972 by President Richard Nixon. He is also the cofounder of the National Conference of Black Lawyers. Hastie became the first African American federal judge when he was appointed by President Franklin D. Roosevelt to the U.S. District Court for the Virgin Islands in 1937. He was also the first African American Governor of the Virgin Islands and was appointed by President Harry S. Truman to the U.S. Court of Appeals for the Third Circuit. This latter appointment made him the first African American appellate judge. Hayes became the first African American to serve on the District of Columbia Public Utilities Commission. Greenberg served as director of the NAACP Legal Defense Fund from 1961 until 1984, argued 40 civil rights cases before the Supreme Court, and later taught at Columbia University's Law School. He received the Presidential Citizens Medal from President Bill Clinton in 2001. Hill practiced law for 60 years, became the first African American on the city council of Richmond since Reconstruction in 1949, and was awarded the Presidential Medal of Freedom by President Bill Clinton in 1999. These are just some of the accomplishments of all these extraordinary protégés of Houston.

Houston began to tour the South with a camera and portable typewriter to get a first-hand view of segregation and discrimination. The conditions that were especially prevalent in the South, but also in many Northern areas, were the result of Jim Crow laws. These laws resulted from legal and social resistance to laws passed by the federal government after the Civil War to end discrimination against African Americans. This resistance included segregating or banning blacks and whites from attending the same schools, eating in the same restaurants, staying in the same hotels, and using the same forms of transportation. Even when they were allowed to use the same facilities, areas were sectioned off according to race to ensure blacks were subjected to inferior conditions. In addition, state governments intentionally gave higher levels of funding to schools, facilities, organizations, and agencies that

supported whites. Blacks were restricted from voting, sitting on juries, and serving in certain government positions in order to maintain the superiority of whites. Jim Crow laws established a culture of discrimination and those who violated them were often subject to harsh and swift punishment.

The term *Jim Crow* originated in the 1820s when a white entertainer named Thomas "Daddy" Rice copied a song and dance routine from a black man named Jim Crow. Rice blackened his face, dressed himself to look like Crow, and became famous for his blackface act. By the end of the 1800s, the name Jim Crow was used as a racist stereotype of blacks and also applied to laws that discriminated against blacks (Horn, 2004, p. 5).

Thurgood often accompanied Houston on trips to the South and later recalled, "There was no place to eat, no place to sleep. We slept in the car and we ate fruit" (Smith, 2003, p. 279). However, Houston and Thurgood endured these challenges because these trips were part of Houston's strategy to challenge "separate but equal" by documenting the substandard conditions of facilities for blacks. Houston reasoned that court challenges against states that created or supported these conditions would result in these states being forced to fund drastic improvements to black facilities or integration. This was the basis of his equalization strategy. In the fall of 1934, Houston rented a handheld camera and filmed blacks living in rural South Carolina. Part of the funds that paid for the film was from the Harmon Foundation of New York. The foundation was established by a white real estate developer from New York to promote racial tolerance. The film detailed racial segregation in schools, the predominance of illiteracy in the black community, and blacks living in extreme poverty. The film is preserved at the National Archives and Records Administration in College Park, Maryland.

The first NAACP case to challenge a state was against Maryland as Thurgood had wanted. Houston wanted to take the Murray case as part of his plan to challenge Jim Crow laws in the courts, starting with cases involving qualified blacks who had been denied admission to graduate and professional schools and unequal pay for black teachers. In 1935, Donald Gaines Murray Sr., a graduate of the historically black Amherst University, was refused admission by the University of Maryland's law

school because he was black, and his appeal to the school's Board of Regents was unsuccessful. The rejection from the university simply stated, "the University does not accept Negro students," and he was referred to Howard University's law school. When he applied again and was not admitted, he obtained legal representation from Thurgood and Houston. The case was originally brought to Houston's attention by William Gosnell, counsel for Alpha Phi Alpha Fraternity, Inc. Thurgood and Houston filed a petition in the Maryland state court on April 8, 1935, asking that the Board of Regents be directed to admit Murray.

In court, Thurgood argued that "since the State of Maryland had not provided a comparable law school for blacks that Murray should be allowed to attend the white university. . . . What's at stake here is more than the rights of my client. It's the moral commitment stated in our country's creed" (University of Maryland School of Law, 2011). Judge Eugene O'Dunne ordered Raymond A. Pearson, president of the university, to admit Murray and the ruling was upheld when appealed to Maryland's highest court, the Court of Appeals, on January 15, 1936 (*Raymond A. Pearson v. Donald G. Murray*, 169 Md. 478, (1936)). In its ruling, the court stated, "Compliance with the Constitution cannot be deferred at the will of the state. Whatever system is adopted for legal education now must furnish equality of treatment now." It was not expected that Thurgood and Houston would win their case, but they did. They even expected they would lose and then be able to appeal the case to the Supreme Court. While arguing the case, Thurgood displayed what would become his trademark oratory style of straightforwardness and plain speaking. For example, when he was asked to define *equal* by Justice Frankfurter, Thurgood replied, "equal means getting the same thing, at the same time and in the same place."

After the Murray case, Thurgood became a full-time lawyer for the NAACP. He left Baltimore and went with Houston back to New York to become the organization's Chief Counsel. Based on a brief written by Thurgood, Houston filed a lawsuit against the state of Missouri for refusing to admit African American students to the state university's law school. The state instead offered students the option of going to an out-of-state school or attending a separate African American law school the state had not yet established. Lloyd Gaines, a graduate from Missouri's state-supported black school, Lincoln University of Missouri,

was denied admission to the law school at the University of Missouri. The university noted that if he chose to take advantage of an out-of-state scholarship program, the state would pay his expenses to attend anywhere Negroes were accepted. In *Missouri ex rel. Gaines v. Canada*, 305 U.S. 337 (1938), the state courts ruled against the NAACP. The case was appealed and almost three years later the U.S. Supreme Court ruled that the University of Missouri had to admit Gaines because the state did not provide access to legal training for its African American citizens. The Court argued that equal protection clause of the Fourteenth Amendment required the state to provide equal educational opportunities and facilities. The state began to upgrade Lincoln University and established a law school for blacks there but drastically underfunded the school in comparison to the University of Missouri. The case ended when Gaines disappeared. In March 1939 he left his home, telling the door attendant he was going to buy stamps. He was never seen again and no suspects in his disappearance were ever identified.

Thurgood succeeded Houston as head of the NAACP's legal committee in 1938 and became director of the NAACP Legal Defense and Education Fund, serving in this position from 1940 until 1961. The legal office separately reorganized from the rest of the NAACP and became a legal fund to maintain its tax-exempt status. Houston retired in 1940 because of health problems and died on April 22, 1950, of a heart attack at the age of 54. His friends remarked that Thurgood grieved as if he had lost his father. Thurgood later remarked, "We owe it all to Charlie." Houston became known as "The Man Who Killed Jim Crow."

The Legal Defense Fund and the NAACP shared resources, space, and staff until 1957. Thurgood and NAACP Executive Secretary Walter Francis White, worked closely together raising funds and fighting for racial equality. The two did have disagreements at times. Thurgood felt White tried too often to get involved in legal matters. He also felt that while White remained the face of the NAACP, his friend Roy Wilkins (August 30, 1901–September 8, 1981) actually ran the day-to-day operations of the NAACP. Wilkins served as assistant NAACP secretary under White from 1931 until 1934. Wilkins replaced W.E.B. Du Bois as editor of *The Crisis* in 1934 and then chaired the National Emergency Civil Rights Mobilization from 1949 through 1950. In

The 31st annual convention of the NAACP, June 18–23, 1940, Philadelphia, Pennsylvania. (Library of Congress.)

1950, he founded the Leadership Conference on Civil Rights. Wilkins eventually became the NAACP's executive secretary in 1955 and its first executive director in 1964. He was awarded the Presidential Medal of Freedom by President Lyndon Johnson in 1967 due to his leading role in the civil rights movement, his involvement in *Brown v. Board of Education of Topeka*, the passage of the Civil Rights Act of 1964, and the passage of the Voting Rights Act of 1965. Wilkins retired from the NAACP in 1977 and was succeeded by Benjamin Hooks.

African Americans were fighting against several civil rights challenges when Thurgood took his new position. Jim Crow laws were firmly in place in the South. The nation was also entering World War II. Blacks served in the military but were subject to segregation and discrimination. African Americans also continued to migrate to the North for better job opportunities but still faced discrimination and even physical resistance in some cities. Thurgood traveled the country fighting racial segregation. He faced challenges from two fronts. First, his life was often threatened and he was jailed several times. He spoke of one incident during an interview:

> In the '40s, or the '30s, the late '30s. Well I was changing trains and I had about a two or three hour stopover and while I was waiting I got hungry and I saw a restaurant on there so I decided that if I got hungry enough I'd go over there and put my civil rights in my back pocket and go to the back door of the kitchen

and see if I could buy a sandwich. And while I was kibitzing my-self to do that, this white man came up beside me in plain clothes, with a great big pistol in a case on his hip, and he said, Nigger boy, or something, what are you doing here? And I said well I'm wait-ing. And he said what did you say? I said, sir, I'm waiting for the train to Louisiana. Shreveport. And he said, well, there's only one more train comes through here and that's four o'clock and you'd better be on it because the sun is never going down on a live Nig-ger in this town. And you know what? I wasn't hungry anymore I wasn't thinking about eating because it dawned on me he could just blow my head off and he wouldn't even have to go to court. (Horn, 2004, p. 27)

Thurgood's second challenge was criticism by some black individuals and organizations. During the 1940s and 1950s, the Nation of Islam de-nounced Thurgood for supporting integration. The religious organiza-tion of African American Muslims was founded in Detroit, Michigan, in 1930 by Wallace D. Fard Muhammad, whose mission was to improve the economic, spiritual, and social conditions of African Americans. From 1934 through 1975, the organization was led by Elijah Muham-mad. Malcolm X, the organization's prominent minister during the 1950s and 1960s who believed whites were evil and blacks should take aggressive action to force equality, verbally assaulted Thurgood when the two met. Thurgood was advised by New York Police Commis-sioner Stephen Kennedy to carry a gun due to threats Malcolm X had made. However, Thurgood's wife would not allow him to bring a gun into their home. The Nation of Islam was just as critical of Dr. Martin Luther King Jr. In a speech given at Princeton University, Thurgood characterized the Muslims as an organization "run by a bunch of thugs or organized from prisons and jails, and financed, I am sure, by Nasser or some Arab group." Dr. King was somewhat more restrained in his description of the Nation of Islam in a speech he gave before the Na-tional Bar Association. He referred to them as "one of the hate groups arising in our midst which preach a doctrine of black supremacy" (Sha-piro, 1988, p. 466).

Regardless of his criticisms and challenges, Thurgood continued to fight for equal rights for African Americans. Beyond bringing cases to

court, he studied race riots throughout the country from 1940 until he left the NAACP Legal Defense Fund in 1961 in order to publicize the injustices African Americans were facing, particularly by law enforcement officers. One of the most famous riots he studied was one in Detroit, Michigan, in the summer of 1943. Beginning on June 20, 1943, the two-day riot left 34 people dead and led to 1,800 arrests. It began due to the scarcity of housing and jobs for blacks. Many black and white Southerners had swarmed to the city in search of jobs, making munitions for the war. Even though whites were part of the riots, the police basically ignored them and targeted black participants. Thurgood's report criticized the police and the environment that led to the inevitability of the riot taking place. Commenting on that and many other riots, Thurgood stated that riots led to innocent people getting hurt versus those that were guilty.

Thurgood often commented that the most frightening riot he was involved in was in Columbia, Tennessee, in 1946. The riot resulted from a fight between a 19-year-old black World War II veteran, James Stephenson, and a white shopkeeper, Bill Fleming. Stephenson and his mother went to Fleming's shop to complain about a radio that he hadn't fixed. Fleming slapped Stephenson's mother and pushed her out the door. Stephenson punched Fleming who then fell through a window. Fleming went to the hospital and Stephenson was arrested. State troopers and local white citizens destroyed the black business part of the city saying they were looking for hidden weapons. More than 100 black men were arrested, some were charged with attempted murder, and 1 died in the local jail. Thurgood arrived in Columbia three months later with other lawyers to defend blacks who were charged with killing a white man. Fearing for their safety, they had to stay 74 miles away in Nashville during the trial. Thurgood persuaded the judge to move the trial to Lawrenceburg, which wasn't much friendlier to blacks. A sign at the Columbia city line read "Nigger, read and run. Don't let the sun go down on you here. If you can't read, run anyway." They eventually got all but one of the defendants acquitted, remarkably by an all-white jury.

Thurgood became an incredibly successful lawyer on behalf of the NAACP. He won 29 of the 30 cases he argued before the Supreme Court as director of the NAACP Legal Defense and Education Fund,

with the first being *Chambers v. Florida*, 309 U.S. 227 (1940), which he argued when he was 32 years old. He gained a reputation for being thorough in outlining facts in cases and relating them to the law and also in being able to convey his thoughts through storytelling. He also spoke in plain language, addressing issues an ordinary person could relate to. The following are summaries of some of the most notable cases he tried during this period. As can be seen in reading the summaries, Thurgood expanded the NAACP's strategy beyond education to also address segregated facilities because they also isolated and stigmatized African Americans. Public support grew toward the NAACP's efforts and the Justice Department filed briefs supporting some cases.

CHAMBERS V. FLORIDA, 309 U.S. 227 (1940)

Four black men were convicted of robbing and murdering an elderly white man in Pompano Beach, Florida. Chambers and the three co-

NAACP Executive Secretary Roy Wilkins in a press conference with Autherine Lucy and Thurgood Marshall, director and special counsel for the NAACP Legal Defense and Education Fund, 1956. Autherine Lucy was the first African American to attend the University of Alabama. (Library of Congress.)

defendants were 4 of up to 40 black men had been arrested for the murder. Due to outrage from the local community, the 4 men were taken to Miami for questioning and then to Fort Lauderdale. During a week of questioning, they were not informed of their rights, held without being formally charged or arraigned, not allowed to see their lawyer, and often left alone in a room with a crowd of police officers and members of the community. The 4 finally confessed, and were convicted of capital murder and sentenced to death. Their appeal was denied on the grounds that they had confessed voluntarily. After Thurgood argued the case, the Supreme Court overturned the convictions on the grounds that the confessions were coerced and the defendants were denied due process guaranteed by the Fourteenth Amendment. The court also agreed that the confessions were additionally gained through the application of physical violence and torture, which was a common practice used by police officers in the South at the time.

SMITH V. ALLWRIGHT, 321 U.S. 649 (1944)

Lonnie E. Smith, a black voter in Harris County, Texas, sued county election official S. S. Allwright for the right to vote in a primary election being held by the Democratic Party in 1940. The law at the time allowed the party to only admit white voters. Most elections in the South were decided by the outcome of Democratic Party elections because they had controlled politics in the South since the late 1800s. The Texas Supreme Court contended that the party was a "voluntary association" and could set its own rules for membership. After Thurgood presented arguments, the Supreme Court overturned the decision it made in *Grovey v. Townsend,* 295 U.S. 45 (1935) that Democratic Party primaries were private affairs and not subject to state regulation. In *Smith* it ruled the party's practice in Texas and other states denied all citizens equal protection under the law. Even though the party was a voluntary organization, it conducted business under state statutory authority, fell under the auspices of rulings made in state courts, and the results of primary elections governed the selection of public officials. The party was also ordered to pay Smith $5,000 in compensatory damages.

MORGAN V. VIRGINIA, 328 U.S. 373 (1946)

In 1944, 27-year-old Irene Morgan refused to give up her seat to a white person on a Greyhound bus in Virginia. The bus driver stopped the bus in Middlesex County, Virginia and called the sheriff. When the sheriff tried to arrest her, Morgan tore up the arrest warrant, kicked the sheriff in the groin and fought with the deputy who tried to drag her off the bus. When the case was finally appealed from the lower courts to the Supreme Court, the high court ruled on behalf of Morgan and struck down laws requiring segregation in interstate transportation. The court agreed with Thurgood's argument that segregation in interstate travel violated the Commerce Clause of the Constitution. The ruling in the Morgan case had further future impacts. In 1947, 16 members of the Chicago-based Congress of Racial Equality (CORE) rode interstate buses throughout the South to test the enforcement of the Supreme Court's decision. During their "Journey of Reconciliation," CORE activists did not face opposition in Virginia but faced violence and arrests in North Carolina. Activist Bayard Rustin was sentenced to 22 days on a chain gang in the South. In 1960, the Supreme Court extended its decision in *Morgan* to bus terminals used in interstate service in *Boynton v. Virginia*, 364 U.S. 454 (1960). The Journey of Reconciliation inspired CORE to organize the Freedom Rides of 1961 to also test the enforcement of the Supreme Court's decision in *Boynton*. The violence and arrests that resulted throughout the South brought national attention to the issue. In 2001, Irene Morgan was awarded the Presidential Citizens Medal by President Bill Clinton.

PATTON V. MISSISSIPPI, 332 U.S. 463 (1947)

Thurgood argued the case as the result of an African American, Eddie Patton, who had been indicted for murder by an all-white grand jury. While one-third of the population in Lauderdale County, Mississippi was African American and there were at least 25 qualified African American eligible to serve, none were chosen. No African Americans had served on a jury in the county for 30 years. The state had maintained that the exclusion of blacks was justified because so few were qualified to vote. The Supreme Court ruled that the exclusion of

African Americans from serving on juries was in violation of the Equal Protection Clause of Fourteenth Amendment.

SHELLEY V. KRAEMER, 334 U.S. 1 (1948)

In 1945, the Shelley family purchased a house in St. Louis, Missouri but was unaware that a restrictive covenant established in 1911 barred blacks from the owning property. Louis Kramer lived 10 blocks from the house and sued to restrain the Shelleys from taking possession of the house. The Supreme Court of Missouri ruled the covenant was legal because it was established as a private agreement by the original owners of the house. A similar case was being heard in Detroit, Michigan in *Sipes v. McGhee*, 316 Mich. 615 (1947) after the McGhee family purchased land banned by a similar restrictive covenant. When each case reached the Supreme Court, they were combined. In agreement with Thurgood's argument, the court ruled that state enforcement of racially based restrictive covenants violated the Equal Protection Clause of the Fourteenth Amendment.

SIPUEL V. UNIVERSITY OF OKLAHOMA, 332 U.S. 631 (1948) AND SWEATT V. PAINTER, 339 U.S. 629 (1950)

Ada Lois Sipuel was not allowed to attend the only state-supported law school in Oklahoma. She was African American and advised that the state was building a separate and equal facility for blacks in the near future. The state provided an out-of-state scholarship for black citizens to attend professional and graduate schools elsewhere. During the trial, Thurgood brought in professors from leading law schools to testify in district court. Professors from Harvard University, the University of Chicago, the University of Wisconsin, and Columbia University testified that separate law schools without diverse student bodies promulgated an unequal and inadequate legal education. The court, however, ruled that the university did not have to open a law school until enough black applicants showed interest to make providing a separate facility practical. The case was appealed to the Oklahoma Supreme Court but the court upheld the district court's decision. The NAACP appealed to

the Supreme Court and was joined by the National Lawyers Guild and the ACLU. They collectively argued that segregated higher education systems perpetuated a caste system that made equality of the races unattainable. The Supreme Court handed down a unanimous decision that Oklahoma had to provide a legal education for Sipuel. The same ruling was handed down two years later in a parallel case, *Sweatt v. Painter*, 339 U.S. 629 (1950), in which Heman Marion Sweatt was refused admission to the University of Texas School of Law on the grounds that the Texas State Constitution prohibited integrated education.

MCLAURIN V. OKLAHOMA STATE REGENTS, 339 U.S. 637 (1950)

George W. McLaurin was denied admission to the University of Oklahoma's Doctor of Education program. The U.S. District Court for the Western District Court of Oklahoma ruled in favor of McLaurin and agreed the university was in violation of his Fourteenth Amendment rights. Although state law prohibited blacks and whites from attending school together, the three-judge panel also found no separate facilities had been established for blacks. The court did not issue any injunctive relief, so the university provided him separate accommodations that included a special table in the cafeteria, a desk outside of the classroom doorway, and a separate desk in the library. McLaurin appealed to the U.S. District Court on the grounds that he was not allowed to interact with other students. After the district court denied his petition, the case was appealed to the Supreme Court. The court ruled the university had to remove any restrictions to McLaurin. Chief Justice Fred M. Vinson, writing for the court, held that the differential treatment given to McLaurin was in violation of the Equal Protection Clause of the Fourteenth Amendment and stated "such restrictions impair and inhibit his ability to study, to engage in discussions and exchange views with other students, and, in general, to learn his profession" (*McLaurin v. Okla. St. Regents for Higher Ed.*, 339 U.S. 637 (1950), at 641). This case was decided the same day as *Sweatt v. Painter*, 339 U.S. 629 (1950) and effectively ended "separate but equal" in graduate and professional education. It also signaled that the Supreme Court would not only rule in favor of segregated education.

All of the above lawsuits were challenges resulting from the
NAACP's equalization plan. During an interview with American Ra-
dioWorks, Roy Wilkins stated of Thurgood and Houston that they
"challenged both the factual equality between the black and the white
schools, as well as the general principle that separate could be equal
in some meaningful constitutional sense. . . . Each victory then built
up to the next victory and the next victory, and by the late 1940s they
had won a series of cases. *Brown* was the culmination of that 20-year
campaign" (Smith and Ellis, 2011).

The plan of the NAACP was instituted at a time when the ideology
of the justice system was changing. During the administration of Presi-
dent Franklin D. Roosevelt, the historical nonintervention stance of
the Supreme Court on state laws changed. Instead, the majority opin-
ion of the justices was that human and civil rights should be preserved

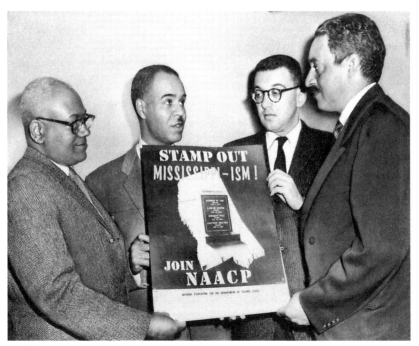

*Holding a poster in 1956 against racial bias in Mississippi are four of the most
active leaders in the NAACP movement, from left: Henry L. Moon, director of
public relations; Roy Wilkins, executive secretary; Herbert Hill, labor secretary;
and Thurgood Marshall, special counsel.* (World Telegram & Sun *photo by Al
Ravenna. Library of Congress.*)

and that the Bill of Rights applied to all citizens. This change in position resulted from the appointment of four judges: Hugo Black in 1937, Stanley Reed in 1938, Frank Murphy in 1940, and Robert Jackson in 1941.

Thurgood discussed the struggle for equal rights and the plan of the NAACP during a speech given at the NAACP Wartime Conference in Chicago, Illinois on July 13, 1942. The following is an excerpt from that speech, entitled "The Legal Attack to Secure Civil Rights":

The struggle for full citizenship rights can be speeded by enforcement of existing statutory provisions protecting our civil rights. The attack on discrimination by use of legal machinery has only scratched the surface. An understanding of the existing statutes protecting our civil rights is necessary if we are to work towards enforcement of these statutes. . . . The Fourteenth and Fifteenth Amendments to the Constitution are prohibitions against action by the states and state officers violating civil rights. In addition to these provisions of the United States Constitution and a few others, there are several statutes of the United States which also attempt to protect the rights of individual citizens against private persons as well as public officers. . . . All of the statutes, both federal and state, which protect the individual rights of Americans are important to Negroes as well as other citizens. Many of these provisions, however, are of peculiar significance to Negroes because of the fact that in many instances these statutes are the only protection to which Negroes can look for redress. It should also be pointed out that many officials of both state and federal governments are reluctant to protect the rights of Negroes. It is often difficult to enforce our rights when they are perfectly clear. It is practically impossible to secure enforcement of any of our rights if there is any doubt whatsoever as to whether or not a particular statute applies to the particular state of facts. Despite the purposes of these Acts which the United States Supreme Court insisted in 1879 "make the rights and responsibilities, civil and criminal, of the two races exactly the same," the experience of all of us points to the fact that this purpose has not as yet been accomplished. There are several reasons for this. In the first place,

in certain sections of this country, especially in the deep South, judges, prosecutors and members of grand and petit juries, have simply refused to follow the letter or spirit of these provisions. Very often it happens that although the judge and prosecutor are anxious to enforce the laws, members of the jury are reluctant to protect the rights of Negroes. A third reason is that many Negroes themselves for one reason or another hesitate to avail themselves of the protection afforded by the United States Constitution and statutes. The most important of the civil rights provisions is the one which provides that "every person who, under color of any statute, ordinance, regulation, custom or usage of any state or territory subjects or causes to be subjected any citizen of the United States or person within the jurisdiction thereof to the deprivation of any rights, privileges, or immunities secured by the Constitution and laws shall be liable to the party injured in an action at law, suit in equity or other proper proceeding for redress." Under this statute any officer of a state, county or municipality who while acting in an official capacity, denies to any citizen or person within the state any of the rights guaranteed by the Constitution or laws is subject to a civil action. This statute has been used to equalize teachers' salaries and to obtain bus transportation for Negro school children. It can be used to attack every form of discrimination against Negroes by public school systems. The statute has also been used to enjoin municipalities from refusing to permit Negroes to take certain civil service examinations and to attack segregation ordinances of municipalities. It can likewise be used to attack all types of discrimination against Negroes by municipalities as well as by states themselves. . . . However, the NAACP is in the process of preparing a detailed memorandum and will establish procedure which will lead to an all-out legal attack on restrictive covenants. Whether or not this attack will be successful cannot be determined at this time.

Because of his achievements as lawyer, Thurgood received the NAACP's Spingarn Medal in 1946. The award was established by Chairman of the Board of the NAACP Joel Elias Spingarn in 1914, and is given annually to an African American to recognize outstanding

achievement. Winners who won the award before Thurgood included W.E.B. Du Bois, George Washington Carver, Charles W. Chestnutt, Mary McLeod Bethune, Marian Anderson, William H. Hastie, and Charles R. Drew. Winners since Thurgood have included Charles Hamilton Houston, Dr. Martin Luther King Jr., Duke Ellington, Langston Hughes, Roy Wilkins, Leontyne Price, Andrew Young, Rosa Parks, Oprah Winfrey, Maya Angelou, and Cicely Tyson.

Chapter 3

BROWN V. BOARD OF EDUCATION OF TOPEKA

Brown v. Board of Education of Topeka, 347 U.S. 483 (1954) is arguably Thurgood's and the NAACP's most important victory in their desegregation campaign and the most significant U.S. Supreme Court decision on race and education. Some have called the case the most influential of the 20th century. It undeniably established the legal foundation for the civil rights movement of the 1950s and 1960s, and led to the passage of the Civil Rights Act of 1964, the Voting Rights of 1965 and the Fair Housing Act of 1968. The NAACP was successful in beginning to completely reverse discriminatory practices that had existed in the United States since the nation was founded.

Oliver L. Brown was one of the plaintiffs of the 13 parents of 20 children from Kansas, and his name appeared first in court filings. The other plaintiffs were Darlene Brown, Lena Carper, Sadie Emmanuel, Marguerite Emerson, Shirley Fleming, Zelma Henderson, Shirley Hodison, Maude Lawton, Alma Lewis, Iona Richardson, and Lucinda Todd. Each had tried to enroll their children in white schools. Brown tried to enroll his daughter, Linda, at Summer Elementary School which was seven blocks from their home but for whites only. The school for black children was a mile away, and his third grade daughter had to walk there and

*Thurgood Marshall, right, special counsel for the NAACP, and Wiley Branton,
Little Rock NAACP attorney, circa 1957. (Library of Congress.)*

cross a railroad switchyard on the way. Brown was convinced to join the
lawsuit by his childhood friend Charles Scott who was one of the leaders
of the Topeka branch of the NAACP. The NAACP lawyers sought to
invalidate a Kansas statute (Kansas General Statute Section 72-1724
(1949)) which permitted cities of more than 15,000 people to maintain
separate school facilities for Negro and white students.

The case was first heard by the U.S. District Court for the District of
Kansas from June 25, 1951 through June 26, 1951. The NAACP, repre-
senting Brown and the other plaintiffs, argued that segregated schools
send the message to black children that they were inferior to whites,
and the schools themselves were thus inherently unequal. They used
expert witnesses to support their case. For example, Dr. Hugh W. Speer,
chairman of the Department of Education at the University of Kansas
City, testified that "if the colored children are denied the experience
in school of associating with white children, who represent 90 percent
of our national society in which these colored children must live, then
the colored child's curriculum is being greatly curtailed. The Topeka

curriculum or any school curriculum cannot be equal under segregation" (Williams, 1987, p. 24).

The defense for the Topeka Board of Education countered that segregation was a part of American life and, therefore, segregated schools prepared children for what they would face during adulthood. The three-judge District Court panel concurred that segregation had a detrimental effect on black children, but ruled in favor of the school system because of the Supreme Court's ruling in *Plessy v. Ferguson*, 163 U.S. 537 (1896) and no subsequent rulings that had overturned it. Per the requirements of *Plessy*, the panel also held that Negro and white schools were substantially equal with respect to buildings, transportation, curricula, and educational qualifications of teachers.

The NAACP appealed the case to the Supreme Court on October 1, 1951, and it was combined with other cases in South Carolina, Virginia, and Delaware. By this time, Thurgood was 44 years old. He had argued 15 cases before the Supreme Court and won 13 of them. The lead attorney for the defending Southern states was John W. Davis. Davis was 79 years old, and had been a Democratic congressman and presidential nominee. He had also participated in 250 Supreme Court cases, more than anyone else in the nation at that time.

The case was first argued on December 9, 1952, but the Supreme Court could not reach a decision. Associate Justice Felix Frankfurter asked for the case to be reargued as a stalling tactic that he hoped would result in a unanimous decision to rule in favor of the plaintiffs. However, Chief Justice Fred M. Vinson supported segregation and tried to convince the other Justices to vote in favor of the defendants. Vinson died in September 1953 before the case could be reheard. President Dwight D. Eisenhower appointed Earl Warren as Chief Justice. Warren supported school integration. While serving as the governor of California, he signed into law a repeal of the state's segregationist provisions in California statutes. This resulted from California district court rulings in *Mendez, et al v. Westminster School District, et al*, 64 F.Supp. 544 (C.D. Cal. 1946), aff'd, 161 F.2d 774 (9th Cir. 1947) that held the segregation of Mexican students in Orange County, California schools was unconstitutional. Warren convinced his fellow justices that the court had to unanimously agree on the *Brown* cases to avoid Southern

resistance, hand down a ruling that would be evidence the court legally viewed blacks and whites as equals, and overturn *Plessy v. Ferguson* to maintain the court's legitimacy. After rehearing the case, it was decided by the Supreme Court on May 17, 1954.

Chief Justice Warren summarized the case in providing the unanimous opinion of the court. In the South Carolina case, *Briggs v. Elliott*, the plaintiffs were Negro children of both elementary and high-school age from Clarendon County. They brought this action in the U.S. District Court for the Eastern District of South Carolina to enjoin enforcement of provisions in the state constitution and statutory code which require the segregation of Negroes and whites in public schools. The three-judge District Court found that the Negro schools were inferior to the white schools and ordered the defendants to begin immediately to equalize the facilities but sustained the validity of the contested provisions and denied the plaintiffs admission to the white schools during the equalization program. The Supreme Court had already remanded the case back to the District Court to obtain progress on the equalization program. On remand, the District Court found that substantial

Lawyers for the National Association for the Advancement of Colored People celebrate outside the Supreme Court after successfully challenging school segregation in Brown v. Board of Education *(1954). From left to right are: George E. Hayes, Thurgood Marshall, and James Nabrit. (Library of Congress.)*

equality had been achieved except for buildings and that the defendants were proceeding to rectify this inequality as well.

In the Virginia case, *Davis v. County School Board*, the plaintiffs were Negro children of high-school age residing in Prince Edward County. They brought this action in the U.S. District Court for the Eastern District of Virginia to enjoin enforcement of provisions in the state constitution and statutory code which require the segregation of Negroes and whites in public schools. The three-judge District Court found the Negro school inferior in physical plant, curricula, and transportation, and ordered the defendants forthwith to provide substantially equal curricula and transportation and to "proceed with all reasonable diligence and dispatch to remove" the inequality in physical plant. But, as in the South Carolina case, the court sustained the validity of the contested provisions and denied the plaintiffs admission to the white schools during the equalization program.

In the Delaware case, *Gebhart v. Belton*, the plaintiffs were Negro children of both elementary and high-school age residing in New Castle County. They brought this action in the Delaware Court of Chancery to enjoin enforcement of provisions in the state constitution and statutory code which require the segregation of Negroes and whites in public schools. The chancellor gave judgment for the plaintiffs and ordered their immediate admission to schools previously attended only by white children on the ground that the Negro schools were inferior with respect to teacher training, pupil-teacher ratio, extracurricular activities, physical plant, and time and distance involved in travel. The chancellor's decree was affirmed by the Supreme Court of Delaware, which intimated, however, that the defendants might be able to obtain a modification of the decree after equalization of the Negro and white schools had been accomplished. The defendants, contending only that the Delaware courts had erred in ordering the immediate admission of the Negro plaintiffs to the white schools, appealed the case.

In each of the cases, the lawyers for the plaintiffs alleged the children were denied equal protection of the laws under the Fourteenth Amendment. In each of the cases other than the Delaware case, a three-judge federal District Court denied relief to the plaintiffs on the "separate but equal" doctrine established in *Plessy v. Ferguson*, 163 U.S. 537. In the Delaware case, the Supreme Court of Delaware adhered to

that doctrine, but ordered that the plaintiffs be admitted to the white schools because of their superiority to the Negro schools. The plaintiffs contended that segregated public schools are not equal and cannot be made equal, and that hence they are deprived of the equal protection of the laws.

The court analyzed segregation and "separate but equal" doctrine based upon the effect of segregation itself on public education and "public education in the light of its full development and its present place in American life throughout the nation. Only in this way can it be determined if segregation in public schools deprives these plaintiffs of the equal protection of the laws." The court found that, "Today, education is perhaps the most important function of state and local governments. Compulsory school-attendance laws and the great expenditures for education both demonstrate our recognition of the importance of education to our democratic society. It is required in the performance of our most basic public responsibilities, even service in the armed forces. It is the very foundation of good citizenship. Today it is a principal instrument in awakening the child to cultural values, in preparing him for later professional training, and in helping him to adjust normally to his environment. In these days, it is doubtful that any child may reasonably be expected to succeed in life if he is denied the opportunity of an education. Such an opportunity, where the state has undertaken to provide it, is a right which must be made available to all on equal terms."

The court then tried the case based upon the question, "Does segregation of children in public schools solely on the basis of race, even though the physical facilities and other 'tangible' factors may be equal, deprive the children of the minority group of equal educational opportunities?" The court ruled that it did. Referring to its prior rulings in *Sweatt v. Painter* and *McLaurin v. Oklahoma State Regents* that intangible considerations must be applied, the court ruled that "separating children in grade and high school from others of similar age and qualifications solely because of their race generates a feeling of inferiority as to their status in the community that may affect their hearts and minds in a way unlikely ever to be undone. . . . Segregation with the sanction of law, therefore, has a tendency to [retard] the educational and mental development of Negro children and to deprive them of some of the

benefits they would receive in a racial(ly) integrated school system (see Appendix for full case)." The court struck down the "separate but equal" doctrine it established in *Plessy v. Ferguson* as unconstitutional because it violated the due process clause of the Fourteenth Amendment.

The Supreme Court was influenced by several documents in their ruling in *Brown*. One was a report issued by the United Nations Educational, Scientific and Cultural Organization (UNESCO) on July 20, 1950, entitled *The Race Question*. The report was signed by a variety of internationally renowned scholars. It condemned racism as morally wrong and denounced past attempts to scientifically justify racism. For example, the report ended by stating

> biological studies lend support to the ethic of universal brotherhood; for man is born with drives toward co-operation, and unless these drives are satisfied, men and nations alike fall ill. Man is born a social being who can reach his fullest development only through interaction with his fellows. The denial at any point of this social bond between men and man brings with it disintegration. In this sense, every man is his brother's keeper. For every man is a piece of the continent, a part of the main, because he is involved in mankind. (UNESCO, 1969, p. 35)

Among those who drafted the document were Professors Franklin Frazier (United States), Morris Ginsberg (United Kingdom), Ernest Beaglehole (New Zealand), and Dr. Humayun Kabia (India).

The Supreme Court also cited *An American Dilemma: The Negro Problem and Modern Democracy* written by Gunnar Myrdal. The 1944 book discusses the dichotomy of African Americans being loyal to a nation whose founding *creed* is based on the guarantee of a national creed of inalienable rights, and freedom and justice for all while at the same time they daily face racial discrimination and segregation. One passage from the book states, "The American Negroes know that they are a subordinated group experiencing, more than anybody else in the nation, the consequences of the fact that the Creed is not lived up to in America. Yet their faith in the Creed is not simply a means of pleading their unfulfilled rights. They, like the whites, are under the spell of the great national suggestion. With one part of themselves they actually

believe, as do the whites, that the Creed is ruling America" (Myrdal, 1994, p. 4). Myrdal was also one of the signatories of the UNESCO's *The Race Question*.

The U.S. District Court for the District of Kansas appealed the ruling in the 1954 *Brown* decision and the Supreme Court heard and issued further instructions in *Brown v. Board of Education*, 349 U.S. 294 (1955), referred to as *Brown II*. Chief Justice Warren again delivered the unanimous opinion of the court on May 31, 1955. He reiterated that racial discrimination in public education was unconstitutional and all provisions of federal, state, or local law requiring or permitting such discrimination had to yield to this principle. The court ruled that, "School authorities have the primary responsibility for elucidating, assessing, and solving these problems; [district] courts will have to consider whether the action of school authorities constitutes good faith implementation of the governing constitutional principles. Because of their proximity to local conditions and the possible need for further hearings, the courts which originally heard these cases can best perform this judicial appraisal. Accordingly, we believe it appropriate to remand the cases to those courts." The states were ordered to eliminate obstacles to following the court's order in a systematic and effective manner, but were allowed time to comply. Specifically, the district courts were given the authority to

> consider problems related to administration, arising from the physical condition of the school plant, the school transportation system, personnel, revision of school districts and attendance areas into compact units to achieve a system of determining admission to the public schools on a nonracial basis, and revision of local laws and regulations which may be necessary in solving the foregoing problems. They will also consider the adequacy of any plans the defendants may propose to meet these problems and to effectuate a transition to a racially nondiscriminatory school system. During this period of transition, the courts will retain jurisdiction of these cases. (*Brown v. Board of Education*, 349 U.S. 294 (1955))

Many Southern states did not immediately end educational segregation after the Supreme Court's rulings. In Virginia, Senator Harry F.

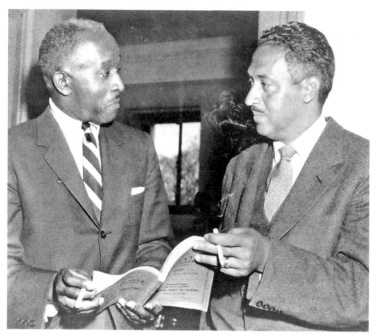

Attorney Louis L. Redding, left, and Thurgood Marshall, general counsel for NAACP, conferring at the Supreme Court during a recess in the court's hearing on racial integration in public schools, 1955. (Library of Congress.)

Byrd Sr. organized the Massive Resistance movement on February 24, 1956, which included withholding state funds from any school that integrated, giving the governor the power to close schools rather than allowing them to be desegregated, and giving tuition grants to white students to attend private white schools of their choice. The NAACP followed with lawsuits to combat Virginia's actions, which then resulted in Governor James Lindsey Almond Jr. closing Warren County High School, schools in Charlottesville, and six schools in Norfolk. Virginia did not fully integrate its schools until the late 1980s.

In 1956, all 101 congressmen in the deep South signed the *Southern Manifesto*, which stated the Supreme Court's rulings were a clear abuse of judicial power and the federal government had no power to force the states to integrate their schools without violating the states' rights per the Constitution's mandate for checks and balances between the federal and state governments. The idea for the manifesto was conceived by South Carolina's Senator Strom Thurmond who enlisted the aid of

Virginia's Senator Byrd. The final version of the document was mostly written by Georgia Senator Richard Russell. It was signed by 82 Southern members of the House of Representatives and 19 Southern senators. The congressional members represented Alabama, Arkansas, Florida, Georgia, Louisiana, Mississippi, North Carolina, South Carolina, Tennessee, Texas, and Virginia. It specifically stated, "Even though we constitute a minority in the present Congress, we have full faith that a majority of the American people believe in the dual system of government which has enabled us to achieve our greatness and will in time demand that the reserved rights of the States and of the people be made secure against judicial usurpation" (U.S. Congress, 1956, p. 4,515–4,516).

The governor of Arkansas, Orval Faubus, blocked and later closed public schools in Little Rock rather than integrate them. On September 23, 1957, a mob backed by the Arkansas National Guard blocked nine black students from entering all-white Little Rock Central High School. In his speech to the nation on the issue given on September 24, 1957 from the oval office, President Dwight D. Eisenhower declared, "I have today issued an Executive Order directing the use of troops under federal authority to aid in the execution of federal law at Little Rock, Arkansas. . . . Mob rule cannot be allowed to override the decisions of our courts." Approximately 1,000 troops from the U.S. Army's 101st Airborne Division in Fort Campbell, Kentucky were deployed to Little Rock to escort the teenagers (later named the Little Rock Nine) to the school. Eisenhower also federalized the entire 10,000-man Arkansas National Guard, putting them under his control rather than the governor's. The ad hoc Task Force 153rd Infantry was organized at Camp Robinson from national guardsmen from around the state and took over occupying the school when the 101st was withdrawn. The task force remained at the school for the remainder of the school year. Thurgood personally flew to Little Rock in September 1957 and filed suit in federal court. He argued the case before the Supreme Court in *Cooper v. Aaron*, 358 U.S. 1 (1958). The Supreme Court ruled that lower courts could not reverse or change its rulings, and that Arkansas was required to reopen and integrate its schools. Because public officials were required to swear an oath to uphold the Constitution, they had to also abide by the Supreme Court's rulings based on the Constitution. With the support of Governor Faubus, the Arkansas State

Legislature closed the three public high schools for the entire 1958–59 school year rather than integrate them. Thousands of students either left Little Rock to attend school and others enrolled in all-white private schools. Little Rock public schools reopened in the fall of 1959 under an integrated school system. All grade levels in the city were not fully integrated until 1972.

Florida's legislature passed an Interposition Resolution in 1957 that declared the Supreme Court's decision null and void. However, the Governor Thomas LeRoy Collins refused to sign it although he too was against the *Brown* decision. He felt the ruling had to be overturned with legal means rather than a legislative resolution. The governor utilized a provision of the state constitution to unilaterally adjourn the state legislature to prevent the resolution's passage. When the legislature returned, the resolution was passed because the governor could not veto it since it was not a law.

In Alabama, Governor George Wallace personally blocked the door to Foster Auditorium at the University of Alabama in 1963 to prevent two black students from being enrolled. Wallace was a devout opponent of integration as he made clear in his policy of "segregation now, segregation tomorrow, segregation forever" during his campaign for office and 1963 inaugural address. He didn't move until confronted by Deputy U.S. Attorney General Nicolas Katzenbach, federal marshals, and General Henry Graham of the Alabama National Guard. President Kennedy sent the National Guard to the campus to force the admission of the students, Vivian Malone and James Hood.

Presidents Kennedy and Johnson knew that legislation was needed to expand civil rights in all facets of American society for African Americans. The Civil Rights Act of 1964 and Voting Rights Act of 1967 ensured the ruling in *Brown* would be supported by legislation and thus provide the government with the ability to take action against states and individuals who still fought to maintain segregation. President Kennedy introduced the Civil Rights Act in a speech given on June 11, 1963, in which he asked for legislation "giving all Americans the right to be served in facilities which are open to the public—hotels, restaurants, theaters, retail stores, and similar establishments." The new law would allow the U.S. Attorney General to file lawsuits against state governments, which operated segregated schools. After President

Kennedy was assassinated in November 1963, President Johnson pushed for the passage of the new law. In his first address to Congress on November 27, 1963, he stated, "No memorial oration or eulogy could more eloquently honor President Kennedy's memory than the earliest possible passage of the civil rights bill for which he fought so long." There was much congressional debate and strong efforts by Southern congressman to block the bill. The greatest opposition came from Senator Strom Thurmond of South Carolina who stated, "This so-called Civil Rights Proposals, which the President has sent to Capitol Hill for enactment into law, are unconstitutional, unnecessary, unwise and extend beyond the realm of reason. This is the worst civil-rights package ever presented to the Congress and is reminiscent of the Reconstruction proposals and actions of the radical Republican Congress" (Scott, 1963). The bill was eventually passed by Congress and signed by President Johnson on July 2, 1964. Incidentally, both Dr. Martin Luther King Jr. and Malcolm X came to Washington, D.C. to listen to the Senate debate the bill on March 26, 1964. It marked the first and only time the two ever met, and their meeting lasted only for a minute.

On August 6, 1967, President Johnson signed the Voting Rights Act of 1967. The act prohibited the states from requiring "voting qualification or prerequisite to voting, or standard, practice, or procedure . . . to deny or abridge the right of any citizen of the United States to vote on account of race or color." In essence, it ended practices that kept African Americans from voting such as literacy tests in order for a person to register to vote. The Department of Justice was given oversight of how elections were being administered by each state. Any changes to voting procedures by a state had to be precleared by the Department of Justice.

The Supreme Court's order in *Brown II* did not end the issue. In 1978, the case was reopened for a third time. Topeka attorneys Richard Jones, Joseph Johnson, and Charles Scott Jr. (son of an original *Brown* team member), along with the American Civil Liberties Union represented Linda Brown Smith. They argued that the open enrollment policy of the Topeka Public Schools led to further segregation because white parents would send their children to preferred schools. This would create both predominantly African American and predominantly white schools within the same district. In 1989, a three-judge panel of the 10th Circuit found that the vestiges of segregation remained with re-

spect to student and staff assignment. The school district appealed the case to the Supreme Court, but the high Court returned the case to the district court in 1993 for implementation of the ruling handed down by the 10th Circuit Court. A plan developed in 1994 was approved and a bond issue was passed by voters that opened additional elementary magnet schools and redrew district attendance plans. Topeka schools met court standards of racial balance by 1998.

Attorney Jack Greenberg was 79 years old in 1954 when he worked with Thurgood on *Brown v. Board of Education*. In excerpts from an interview with him taken from the U.S. Department of State publication *Justice for All: The Legacy of Thurgood Marshall* (2007), Greenburg stated the following when asked questions by interviewer Alexandra Abboud (a staff editor with the U.S. State Department's Bureau of International Information Programs):

Brown was a school segregation case that said that the laws in place in the Southern part of the United States which prohibited blacks and whites from going to school together were unconstitutional. But more importantly, the *Brown* case was like an ice breaker going through the frozen sea of racism. It broke up the racist system that was essentially congealed into the American polity. We had Southern senators who were elected by whites only, and they kept becoming elected and reelected, and their power depended upon them excluding blacks from political participation. The *Brown* case broke all that up . . . Thurgood Marshall was focused. He always believed in racial integration and wanted to strike down the segregation laws and practices within the United States. I would liken him to General George Marshall during the Second World War. He was the one who got all the troops together from all different areas, competencies, and abilities and melded them into a focused unit. We worked with law professors and practitioners, social psychologists, and historians. He was like the orchestra conductor who brought everyone together and focused them into a single melody.

In 1935, there was a Maryland state case involving the admission of a black student to the University of Maryland Law School that Marshall won. The student was admitted because there was no

law school for blacks. That case never even went to the Supreme Court; it was won in the Maryland state courts. In 1939 there was a case in Missouri which went to the U.S. Supreme Court, and the University of Missouri was ordered to admit a black to the University of Missouri Law School because there was no comparable facility for blacks within the state of Missouri. Then in 1950 there were two cases, one out of Texas and one from Oklahoma. As the Texas case proceeded, the state, seeing the handwriting on the wall, built a law school for blacks. It had two rooms, didn't have a law library, didn't have a law review, had no alumni, but the state argued that was equal, which was a ridiculous claim. And the Supreme Court ruled that there is a lot more than just books, bricks, and the mortar involved in evaluating education. There are the intangibles of your relationships with other students and what you learn from them and the lifelong associations that you make while in school.

In the other case, a black student was excluded from the University of Oklahoma Graduate School of Education. As the case went on, they didn't build another school for him; instead they allowed him to sit in the back of the room just outside the door and look in. Ultimately he was admitted into the classroom and to a seat which was marked for "Negroes only." And the Supreme Court said that (action) separated him from the others in a way that interfered with his ability to learn. So the Court was moving more and more towards recognizing the intangible aspects of education and saying that no matter what you did, you could not be equal so long as you were keeping people separate. In the *Brown* case, the momentum of those earlier cases, or the implication of those cases, was made explicit; separate never could be equal. The work of the LDF (NAACP Legal Defense Fund) showed that law could accomplish a great deal. It was the first public-interest law firm and it institutionalized public-interest law. It won decisions in the Supreme Court saying that the practice of public-interest law is a constitutional right and brought an end to racial segregation. Today, we have this great proliferation of public-interest law firms all over the country, which represent a wide variety of political and social issues.

Because of his success in winning so many cases, Thurgood gained international attention and was often called upon to support other causes, including equal rights causes. By 1955, he was known as "Mr. Civil Rights" and was even featured on the cover of *Time* magazine on September 19, 1955. The feature article stated, "Marshall's feeling of love and awe for the Constitution is exceeded only by his love and awe toward his clients: the Negroes, and especially the Negroes of the South and the border states, who, facing threats of firing, or beating or even death, continue to sign the legal petitions and complaints that must be the starting point of Marshall's cases from the slum and the cotton field to the high and technical levels of the Supreme Court" (*Time* magazine, 1955, p. 25).

Thurgood was asked to take part in many areas outside of the court. He was asked by the United Nations and the United Kingdom to help draft the constitutions of Ghana and Tanzania to protect the rights of white citizens in the two former European colonies when they gained their independence. In the 1940s, Brooklyn Dodgers' general manager Branch Richey asked Thurgood to help Jackie Robinson straighten out his finances. Thurgood gained experience with American public service as early as 1951 when President Harry S. Truman asked him to travel to Japan to investigate the treatment of African American soldiers under the command of General Douglas MacAuthur during the Korean War. Truman issued Executive Order 9981 on July 26, 1948, that integrated the U.S. Military but senior commanders ignored the order. After his visit, Thurgood reported that the Army was practicing segregation and racial discrimination. Every other military branch had already desegregated but MacAuthur refused to comply. In an interview, Thurgood reported on what he found:

There were records of trials, so-called trials, in the middle of the night where the men were sentenced to life imprisonment in hearings that lasted less than ten minutes. They were the old well-known drumhead court-martials, done in the heat of passion and in the heat of war. There were fifty or sixty involved. One death penalty case. I remember in particular: the record showed that this man was charged with being absent in the presence of the enemy. Instead of being charged with AWOL (Absent

Without Leave), he was charged with cowardice in the presence of the enemy. And fortunately for him, he produced two witnesses: a major in the Medical Corps and a lieutenant in the Nurse Corps, both of whom testified that he was in a base hospital the very day that he was supposed to be AWOL. And despite their testimony, he was convicted and given life imprisonment. Just prior to that, I was given an audience with General MacArthur, and I found it very interesting. I questioned him about the continuation of segregation in the Army and he said he was working on it. And I asked him how many years he'd been working on it, and he didn't really remember how many. I reminded him that at the very time we were talking, the Air Force was completely integrated, and the Navy was quite integrated, and the only group not integrated was the Army. He said that he didn't find the Negroes qualified, and when he found them qualified, they would be integrated. (Smith and Ellis, 2011)

After meeting and being so impressed by Thurgood in 1959, Kenyan independence activist Tom Mboya invited him to visit Kenya and help draft the country's new constitution as it was gaining its independence from the United Kingdom. Thurgood's visit in January 1960 grew criticism from officials in the United States and the United Kingdom. Due to British pressure, the Kenyan colonial government did not let Thurgood attend the conference. He then left Kenya and went to London and continued to lobby for Kenya's independence. Thurgood did ultimately draft a bill of rights for the new country that both addressed the needs of the new nation and its minority population comprised of whites and Asians. For example, the preamble stated, "All persons are equal before the law and are entitled without any discrimination or distinction of any kind, such as race, colour, sex, language, religion, political or other opinion, national or social origin, property, birth or other status, to equal protection of the law" (Dudziak, 2008, pp. 310–311). Other parts of the draft addressed freedom of religion, press, association, personal security, voting, education, the right to work, and to join unions. In essence, Thurgood wrote what he wished would have been in place in the United States for all Americans. However, he did not draw upon the U.S. Constitution as a model for Kenya, but

instead from the Universal Declaration of Human Rights which the United Nations' General Assembly adopted on December 10, 1948, based upon the experience of World War II. Other parts of Thurgood's draft were based on the constitutions of Nigeria and Malaya. When the final constitution was developed in 1963, much of Thurgood's draft was included. By then, he was considered a cherished advisor by both Kenyan and Great Britain leaders. The trip changed Thurgood because he was amazed to see racism in Europe was not as prevalent as it was in the United States and he was treated like a scholar. Thurgood's friendship with Mboya is credited for causing the huge number of Kenyan students that came to study in the United States beginning in the 1960s. Thurgood made several more trips to Kenyan over the coming years, establishing a close relationship with Kenyan Prime Minister (and later President) Jomo Kenyatta.

During this time of winning landmark cases and his other accomplishments, Thurgood also faced personal tragedy. His wife Vivian died of cancer in February 1955 on her 44th birthday. She had hidden her condition for months from Thurgood, fearing his knowledge of it would interfere with his work. When he eventually found out, he stayed home with her, cooked meals, and tended to her every needed. After her death a friend said that Thurgood felt his world had come to an end. The two had no children. Vivian suffered several miscarriages during their marriage.

In December 1955, Thurgood married Cecilia "Cissy" Suyat, a former assistant at the NAACP. She was born July 20, 1928, in Puunene, Maui, Hawaii and her parents were among the first immigrants to Hawaii in 1910 from the Philippines Islands. Her life in Hawaii was peaceful and she didn't experience racism or prejudice growing up. Although the state had had people of different races, they integrated well. Cecilia's father owned his own printing company. Her mother died when she was young but Cecilia had many siblings. She moved to New York City in 1948 to live with her maternal aunt and uncle who were completing their Master's degrees at Columbia University. Cecilia attended night classes in court stenography at Columbia and took a job as member of the stenography pool of NAACP. She later recalled the job gave her a "first baptism to the racial challenges" minorities faced in the United States (Jones, 2008). One of her first jobs was to take part in a picket of

a movie theater where *Birth of a Nation* was being shown. The movie depicted black men, who were played by white actors in blackface, as unintelligent and sexually aggressive toward white women. It also depicted the Ku Klux Klan as a heroic organization. After the picket, the theater stopped showing the movie. Cecilia worked her way up to become secretary to the director of branches and field administration at the National NAACP Office in New York, Dr. Gloster Bryant Current (1913–1997), in 1948. This was an important position for Cecilia because Dr. Current was the head of 1,500 NAACP groups across the United States. He reported directly to NAACP Director Walter White. Cecilia did a lot of traveling with Dr. Current. They had to stay in black-only hotels, and hold their conventions and meetings in black churches.

Thurgood and Cecilia met in 1954 and their dating relationship quickly became serious after Vivian died. Because she was Filipino-Hawaiian, Cecilia was concerned an interracial marriage would bring negative attention to Thurgood and the NAACP. She was also concerned about how her own family would react to a Negro son-in-law. Thurgood did not care. After at first saying she would not marry him, eventually Cecilia said yes. The two married on December 17, 1955, at St. Philip's Episcopal Church in Harlem, and they remained married until Thurgood's death in 1993.

Thurgood and Cissy had two children. Thurgood Marshall Jr., the eldest, interned during the summer for Senator Carl Albert of Oklahoma while in high school. He worked for Senator Al Gore while in college, and then served as his legislative liaison to Congress when Gore was vice president. After Thurgood Jr. graduated from the University of Virginia Law School, President Bill Clinton appointed him as special assistant to the president and secretary to the Cabinet. Thurgood Jr. and his wife, Teddi Levy Marshall, were married April 25, 2008, at the Supreme Court and Associate Justice Stephen G. Breyer performed the ceremony. John William Marshall, Thurgood's youngest son, earned a B.A. in government from Georgetown University, and a Post-Baccalaureate Certificate in Administration of Justice from Virginia Commonwealth University. He is a former Virginia state trooper, and U.S. Marshals for the Eastern District of Virginia. In 1999, he was appointed the first African American Director of the U.S. Marshall Service by President Clinton. He served as Virginia Secretary of Pub-

lic Safety under Governors Mark Warner and Tim Kaine from 2002 until 2010.While his two sons were growing up, Thurgood promised he would never punish them for anything wrong he himself had done in life. His wife said Thurgood never did punish his children because there wasn't anything he hadn't done.

During his legal battles against segregation, Thurgood was under surveillance of the Federal Bureau of Investigation beginning in the 1940s and was aware of this. Thurgood and then FBI Director J. Edgar Hoover exchanged several heated letters on the failure of law enforcement to protect the civil rights of African Americans. As a result, Hoover ordered the surveillance of Thurgood and his contacts. Beginning in the 1950s and throughout the 1960s, however, the two developed a secret and friendly relationship due to their mutual dislike of communism. Thurgood credited the improvement in their relationship to Hoover's belief that Thurgood rooted communists out of the NAACP. Thurgood later admitted that he did do this. Both disliked Thomas R. M. Howard, an outspoken civil rights leader from Mississippi who criticized the FBI for not seriously investigating the killings of George W. Lee and Emmitt Till, and other cases. On the Till murder, Howard stated that if "the slaughtering of Negroes is allowed to continue, Mississippi will have a civil war. Negroes are only going to take so much" (Beito and Beito, 2009, p. 117). Thurgood considered Howard a rugged individualist who did not speak for the NAACP. Thurgood's agreement with Hoover forged a closer relationship between the NAACP and the FBI. Thurgood gained Hoover's support for his three later federal appointments. Thurgood even attended a luncheon at the White House held by President Lyndon Johnson to celebrate Hoover's birthday. When asked if he believed Hoover was a racist, Thurgood replied that he never did.

Thurgood was also well aware of Hoover's tactics against Dr. Martin Luther King Jr. Thurgood himself did not agree with King's tactics, believing equal rights for blacks would only be gained in the courts rather than through protests in the streets, even if they were nonviolent. During an interview, Thurgood spoke on Hoover's tactics and Hoover's fear of King as a communist:

He just had an absolute blur on communism. It's unbelievable.
I don't know what happened to him, I don't know what happened

but something happened. No, it was personal. He bugged every-thing King had. Everything. And the guy that did it was a friend of a private detective in New York who's a good friend of mine, Buck Owens. He called up and said, Buck, do you know Martin Luther King? And he said, no. He said do you know anybody that does? He said yes. He said well you please tell him, don't use my name but I'm in the group that's bugging everything he's got. Even when he goes to the toilet. I mean we've bugged everything and I think it's a dirty damn trick and he ought to know about it. So Buck called me and I called Brother King. He was in Atlanta then. And I told him about it and he said, oh forget it, nothing to it. Just didn't interest him. That's what he said. He didn't care, no. (Williams, 1998)

(See copy of *Brown v. Board of Education* Supreme Court case in the Appendix.)

Chapter 4

U.S. COURT OF APPEALS FOR THE SECOND CIRCUIT COURT

Because of his victories in challenging segregation and discrimination before the Supreme Court, President John F. Kennedy appointed Thurgood to the U.S. Court of Appeals for the Second Circuit on September 23, 1961. Thurgood was initially hesitant in accepting the nomination because he feared his supporters would think he was disserting the civil rights movement. He changed his mind because he felt a person should not turn down an opportunity to serve the government. Additionally, an appointment to the Second Circuit was influential because that court was powerful in that it had jurisdiction over New York, Connecticut, and Vermont. It also has appellate jurisdiction over the District of Connecticut, Eastern District of New York, Northern District of New York, Southern District of New York, Western District of New York, and District of Vermont. It is also larger than the other 12 U.S. Courts of Appeals, with 11 active and 13 senior judges.

President Kennedy did not just want to appoint Thurgood because of his legal history. The civil rights movement was gaining strong momentum and the federal government was being called upon to take more aggressive actions to end segregation and combat racial discrimination. Kennedy was reluctant to pass extensive regulations or changes

to laws. Instead, he felt the appointment of African Americans to high positions in the federal government and in judiciary positions would show his support for equal rights. He also knew he had a political obligation to the black community. One of the factors that contributed to Kennedy winning the presidential election in 1960 against Richard Nixon was support from black voters. Kennedy won the election by one-tenth of one percentage point, the closest popular vote margin of any election in the 20th century. However, he won in black communities by wide margins. One reason he was so popular with black voters was his support of Dr. Martin Luther King Jr. when he was arrested in Georgia while leading a civil rights march. Nixon refused to get involved but Kennedy called the local authorities to get King released, and also called King's father and wife. During his campaign, Kennedy made promises to make economic improvements for minorities if elected and voiced his support for civil rights. The support from blacks for Kennedy during the election was the turning point in history when the majority of African Americans started voting Democrat rather than Republican.

Thurgood's road to being appointed began in May 1961 when the House Judiciary Committee sent a list of black nominees to Attorney General Robert Kennedy to fill openings on the federal bench in New York. While Kennedy wanted to appoint African Americans to high positions, it was a tumultuous time for the nation in terms of race relations because of growing unrest mainly in the South. The civil rights movement was becoming more organized due to the efforts of such leaders as Dr. Martin Luther King Jr. and organizations such as the Southern Christian Leadership Conference. At the same time, resistance from Southern local governments, law enforcement agencies and white segregationists was becoming more violent. The civil rights movement was gaining both national and international attention due to violent confrontations in the South.

Among the nominees for the court were Thurgood and Robert Carter. Carter was a former aide of Thurgood and the two became critical of one another. Although Thurgood had gained notoriety as a civil rights lawyer to the point he was called "Mr. Civil Rights," Southern congressmen were more supportive of Carter because he was less controversial. Kennedy initially wanted to place Thurgood on the district

court but Thurgood refused. Robert Kennedy felt that Thurgood would not get appointed to Court of Appeals because he was hated by white segregationists and, therefore, the political cost of trying to appoint Thurgood could be too high. By that time, Bill Hastie, Thurgood's former law professor from Howard University, was serving on the U.S. Court of Appeals for the Third Court and was the highest ranking African American judge in the country. Hastie was nominated by President Harry S. Truman in 1949 and confirmed in 1950. Thurgood wanted to be appointed to the same level. He also did not want to be a trial judge because he felt he had too bad a temper and knew that could lead to his rulings being reversed. Thurgood later told Robert Kennedy directly that he would not accept a district court appointment in a meeting between the two. When Kennedy told him that his appointment would be as a district court judge or nothing, Thurgood replied, "Well, I do understand. The trouble is that you are different from me. You don't know what it means, but all I've had in my life is nothing. It's not new to me, so, goodbye" (*New York Times*, 1993, p. 31). Carter became the front runner for an appointment but was not confirmed after an interview with the judicial committee of the bar association.

Thurgood gained support to be nominated by Louis Martin, the chief black advisor to President Kennedy, deputy chair for minorities for the Democratic National Committee, and a Washington, D.C. newspaper publisher. Martin lobbied directly to Robert Kennedy to get Thurgood appointed to the appeals court rather than the district court. He even enlisted the support of prominent white lawyers and Assistant Attorney General Ramsey Clark to speak on Thurgood's skills. J. Edgar Hoover then sent a memo supporting Thurgood. Robert Kennedy sent the list of eight names of new judges to President Kennedy on September 21, 1961. Robert and John Kennedy timed Thurgood's appointment to be announced a week before the Senate Judiciary Committee was scheduled to recess for the remainder of the year because they anticipated resistance to Thurgood's appointment, especially from those senators supporting segregation. The president could, therefore, make a recess appointment and Thurgood could be acting as a judge before the Senate came back into session.

Thurgood's mother, Norma, died during the time he was waiting to hear about his nomination. She was 74 and had been living in New

York taking care of her sister Denmedia. The time was also difficult for Thurgood because he was working to make sure that Carter did not succeed him as head of the NAACP Legal Defense Fund. Using his influence, Thurgood was successful in getting Jack Greenburg named as his replacement. Greenburg became the only white legal counselor for the NAACP and was appointed in 1961 and served until 1984.

When President Kennedy announced Thurgood's nomination in September, the *New York Times* praised the president's "good judgment" in selecting someone with such "high intelligence, his scrupulous respect for the law and the judicial qualities evident even in his briefs and pleadings" (Tushnet, 1997, p. 10). Thurgood and the other seven nominees were all given recess appointments on October 3, 1961. Because he was not officially appointed by the Senate, he was not given a permanent office and was given low level cases dealing with such topics as taxes and simple corporate law. Still he gained popularity because he was an oddity in the courthouse, being a black judge, and even his secretary, Alice Stovall, gained attention as the first black secretary in the circuit court. Thurgood was also popular because of his personality. He was an excellent storyteller and had a great sense of humor. While the other judges were reserved, Thurgood was informal. He would never close his office door unless he was with another judge.

The Senate Judiciary Committee did prepare for confirmation hearings when it reconvened and it was chaired by James Eastland, a segregationist from Mississippi. Thurgood faced criticism because of his race and the fact that his legal background was only in civil rights. He lacked experience in corporate law and the Second Circuit routinely heard such cases. The Kennedy's resubmitted their nomination to the Senate on January 15, 1962, for the confirmation hearing. Eastland and the other three Senators on the subcommittee of the Judiciary Committee panel delayed hearings several times. Normally hearings for judge are scheduled immediately. Thurgood's hearing was scheduled for April 16 and then postponed until April 24, and then until May 1. Republican Senator Kenneth B. Keating of New York was just one of the many members of Congress who felt the delay inexcusable. He stated, "I propose that this selection be acted upon immediately, for our nation is not so rich in brilliance and talent that we can afford to pigeonhole it, as is being done in the case of Thurgood Marshall" (Alfred, 2005,

p. 87). Soon he was joined by both Republican and Democratic sena-
tors in criticizing the subcommittee, as well as Second Circuit judges
and the public.

Reportedly, Eastland would not consider Thurgood until President
Kennedy also nominated William Harold Cox as a district court judge
in Mississippi. Cox was Eastland's college roommate and also a segre-
gationist. Eastland reportedly told Robert Kennedy, "Tell your brother
that if he will give me Harold Cox, I will give him the nigger [referring
to Thurgood]" (Schlesinger, 1978, p. 308). Cox was appointed, and so
Thurgood's confirmation hearings continued. Six days of hearings were
eventually held but over a three-month period. The hearings focused
on Thurgood's membership with the NAACP, American Civil Liber-
ties Union, and other organizations rather than his qualifications to
serve as a judge. Ultimately he was confirmed after a year of extensive
hearings on September 11, 1962, by a Senate vote of 56 to 14. Thur-
good had been serving as a judge for 11 months but was officially sworn
in on October 23, 1961.

Thurgood was devastated by the assassination of President Kennedy
in 1963. He later stated that at the time he was "going to stop reading
newspapers when I picked up the paper about Kennedy. Nothing but
bad news. That was awful" (Williams, 1998, p. 309). Thurgood con-
centrated on his work. He was making more money and able to spend
more time with his family. To ensure he maintained an appearance of
neutrality, however, he distanced himself from the NAACP. He also
became less active in the civil rights movement, once remarking that
he only knew of the movement by what he read in the newspapers. As
a judge on the court, Thurgood wanted to earn the respect of his col-
leagues so he developed a close relationship with Judge Henry Friendly,
an appointee of President Eisenhower. Friendly was regarded as one of
the nation's best appeals court judges and had been a Wall Street law-
yer. However, Thurgood did not concede his judicial opinions based
upon what Friendly held in a case. Thurgood discussed topics of law
in cases with his clerks before they drafted case summaries for him. In
deciding on cases, he rendered judgments based upon the Constitution
and Supreme Court decisions on similar issues.

Thurgood became more vocal in hearings. In *Keyishian v. Board of
Regents*, 345 F.2d 236, 239 (2d Cir. 1965), he gave the majority ruling

that the teachers could not be required to sign loyalty statements as a condition of their employment. The state wanted teachers to certify in these statements that they were not communists or part of any subversive organization whose intent was to overthrow the government. The Supreme Court later upheld this ruling in 1967. In *Angelet v. Fay*, 333 F.2d 12 (2d Cir. 1964) the plaintiff's apartment was entered by law enforcement officers during a drug bust who didn't have a warrant. At the time of the plaintiff's arrest, federal laws did not prohibit illegal search and seizure. However, stricter federal laws passed since his conviction would have made the use of any evidence when the case first came to court inadmissible. Although the court majority ruling was that new laws could not be retroactively applied, Thurgood disagreed. One of his most notable dissents was in the case of *People of New York v. Galamison*, 342 F.2d 255 (2d Cir. 1965). He took the side of the civil rights protestors who blocked a main road to the New York World's Fair over the poor quality of housing and the lack of jobs for blacks in New York. He also wrote the majority opinion of the court in *Hetenyi v. Wilkins*, 348 F.2d 844 (2d Cir. 1965) that prohibited double jeopardy from being used at the local level when a murder suspect had been tried twice for the same crime in Monroe County, New York.

These and other rulings from Thurgood, as well as his devotion to following the principles of the Constitution, led to President Lyndon B. Johnson considering Thurgood for another appointment. As a circuit judge, Thurgood wrote 118 opinions, including support for academic freedom, the rights of immigrants, limiting government intrusion in cases involving illegal search and seizure, the right to a fair trial, double jeopardy, the right to privacy issues, and the right of civil rights demonstrators to picket and protest. None of his 98 majority opinions were overturned on appeal. Several of his dissenting opinions were later adopted as majority opinions by the Supreme Court. Thurgood was so influential that today the Second Circuit ordinarily houses its clerks' offices and hears oral arguments in the building Thurgood worked, and it has been renamed the Thurgood Marshall U.S. Courthouse in Foley Square in lower Manhattan, New York.

Chapter 5

SOLICITOR GENERAL

President Lyndon Johnson consulted with Attorney General Nicholas Katzenbach about his desire to appoint Thurgood as U.S. solicitor general. The position became available when Archibald Cox, who had served as solicitor general since January 1961, resigned to return to teaching at Harvard University in 1965. Cox later became the first special prosecutor for the Watergate Scandal. Johnson also discussed his plan with African American civil rights leaders that he trusted. Johnson told Roy Wilkins, then the executive director of the NAACP, that he wanted to "build him [Thurgood] up where he is impenetrable," which meant critics would be unable to challenge his qualifications. Johnson's long-term plan was to appoint Thurgood as the first African American to sit on the Supreme Court. Johnson felt that "after two or three years as Solicitor General, he would have added [more cases] to the twenty-nine tough cases that he had as an NAACP attorney, it will make him eminently qualified to become the first Negro Justice" (Branch, 2006, p. 262). Although Johnson knew Southern senators would oppose appointing Thurgood, he wanted to take a major step in undoing the unequal treatment African American citizens had faced and believed Thurgood would serve as a role model for the black

community. As solicitor general, Thurgood would supervise and conduct government litigation in the U.S. Supreme Court. He also felt Thurgood would be an example to whites of how African Americans were fully capable of excelling in high profile government positions. Johnson stated, "I want folks at the U.S. Justice Department to walk down the hall and see a [black person] sitting there" (Davis and Clark, 1992, p. 248). Lastly, Johnson's motives were political. Appointing Thurgood would both strengthen the Democratic Party's support from the African American community and solidify his legacy in American presidential history.

In July 1964, President Johnson called Thurgood and offered him the position. Thurgood replied that he needed time to think it over. Johnson told him to take as much as he needed. Later that evening, Thurgood went home and discussed the offer with his wife and children. When Thurgood returned to work on the next day, he had not reached a definite decision. Around 11 o'clock in the morning, Johnson called and asked if he had made up his mind. When Thurgood said that he thought he had as much as he needed to make a decision, Johnson replied that he'd already had enough time. When Thurgood went the oval office to discuss the particulars of the job, he told the president that by accepting this job it would be almost a $5,000 cut in salary. Johnson informed Thurgood that he was aware of his financial status because he had his income tax statement, bank account information, and financial history documents on his desk. The following details the conversation from Thurgood in an interview he gave to the Lyndon B. Johnson library in 1969 (Baker, 1969):

> He called one day, around this time (July) I think, and I was up in the judges' dining room at the courthouse. My bailiff came up and tapped me on the shoulder. I said, "Fred, what in the world is wrong?" I mean, he's not supposed to bother us at lunch. He was as red as a beet. I said, "What's wrong, Fred?" He said, "The President wants to speak to you. He's on the phone!" I said, "The President of what?" "The President of the United States!" So he had held an elevator, and I went down. Sure enough he was on there. We chatted for about two or three minutes, and he said, "I want you to be my Solicitor General." I said, "Sir?" We chatted

about it, and I said, "Well, Mr. President, I'll have to think this over." He said, "Well, go ahead, but don't tell a living soul." I said, "I assume that means nobody but my wife?" He said, "Yes, that's what I mean by nobody." He said, "Take all the time you want." I said, "Very well, sir." He hung up, and I hung up.

I went home and talked to my wife and we discussed the problems, because one was a lifetime job to trade in for a job at the beckoning of one person. Secondly, it was a $4,500 cut in salary. Third, the living expenses in Washington would be twice what I was paying in New York. So she said okay. We kept thinking about it, and the next day the phone rang. He was on the phone again. I said, "Well, Mr. President, you said I had all the time I needed." He said, "You had it." I said, "Okay." I went down the next morning, and I started telling him these things. He said, "You don't have to tell me. I can tell you everything including what you've got in your bank account. I'm still asking you to make the sacrifice." We talked for quite a while, and I said, "Okay with me."

(Interviewer: Did he explain to you why he wanted you as opposed to just somebody else?) He said he wanted, number one, he wanted me in his Administration. Number two, he wanted me in that spot for two reasons. One, he thought I could handle it. Secondly, he wanted people, young people, of both races to come into the Supreme Court Room, as they all do by the hundreds and thousands, and somebody to say, "Who is that man up there with that swallow tail coat on arguing," and somebody to say, "He's the Solicitor General of the United States." Somebody will say, "But he's a Negro!" He wanted that image, number one. Number two, he thought that he would like to have me as his representative before the Court. The other thing which goes through every conversation we had from then on, he would say at least three or four times, "You know this has nothing to do with any Supreme Court appointment. I want that distinctly understood. There's no quid pro here at all. You do your job. If you don't do it, you go out. If you do it, you stay here. And that's all there is to it."

(Interviewer: He made it clear this did not mean that you would eventually get a Supreme Court appointment?) Over and over again. He made the announcement in the East Room, and

it was very funny when I went in. The press knew nothing about any of this. When I went in he first said that I would come behind Mrs. Johnson, and then he said, "You come and go in right side-by-side with me at the door." We went in together. A murmur went around the press boys, and I found out afterwards that the question they were asking was, "Who has resigned from the Supreme Court?" He made the announcement and then we had the swearing in, and that was that.

Johnson did indeed appoint Thurgood as part of his plan to eventually appoint him to the Supreme Court. In a later conversation with Thurgood, Johnson told him "I want the top lawyer in the United States representing me before the Supreme Court to be a Negro. And be a damn good lawyer that's done it before. So you have those peculiar qualifications. I want to do this job that [Abraham] Lincoln started, and I want to do it the right way" (Coleman et al., 2010)).

Thurgood's confirmation by the Senate was uneventful and nothing like what he went through to get approved for the Second Circuit Court. The solicitor general confirmation hearing took only one month. A 15-minute meeting was held and he was confirmed by a 5–0 vote by the Senate subcommittee, becoming the 33rd U.S. solicitor general and first African American to hold the position on August 11, 1965. He thought he would be able to commute from New York to Washington D.C. He had planned to get an efficiency apartment and live between the two cities because his sons were still in school. Johnson spoke to Thurgood at the swearing in ceremony and bellowed, "What in the hell is this about you commuting?" (Williams, 1998, p. 381). The president promptly told Thurgood to move to Washington D.C., and Thurgood did so shortly after. Thurgood's wife and sons, Supreme Court Associate Justices Hugo L. Black and Tom C. Clark, U.S. Attorney General Nicholas Katzenbach, and J. Edgar Hoover attended Thurgood's swearing in ceremony in the Cabinet room of the White House. In his remarks, Johnson lavished praise on Thurgood and his accomplishments stating:

Since assuming the presidency more than a year and a half ago, I have made a total of 370 major appointments to the federal gov-

ernment. In each of these appointments it has been my goal and my determination to seek out the best qualified man or woman in the nation for the job, regardless of their party or their race or their sex. That goal is fulfilled today as we meet here for the installation of Justice Thurgood Marshall as the 33rd Solicitor General of the United States, and by this act we pay honor to a high office in the American Government, to a man, and, most of all, to the law. Thurgood Marshall symbolizes what is best about our American society: the belief that human rights must be satisfied through the orderly processes of law. At the pinnacle of our system of law is the great Supreme Court of the United States, and the Solicitor General is our first advocate before that great court. So, it is a cause of profound satisfaction to me that in Judge Marshall we shall have an advocate whose lifelong concern has been the pursuit of justice for his fellow man.

I think it might be observed that Thurgood Marshall is the first Negro in the history of the United States ever to become the Solicitor General. Thurgood Marshall is already in the front ranks of the great lawyers of this generation. He has argued 32 cases before the Supreme Court; he has won 29 of them. And that is a batting average of .900. It is likely that should he continue in his present assignment for the next 3 years, that he could very well argue 50 more cases before the highest Court in the land-and that would make him try more cases before the Supreme Court than any man in history had ever presented to that body. But what is more relevant is that his Nation has now progressed to the point-in large measure because of some of the things that he has done-that race really no longer serves as a bar to the exercise of experience, or as a bar to the exercise of one's skills. (The American Presidency Project, 2010)

As solicitor general, Thurgood won 14 of the 19 cases he argued before the Supreme Court on behalf of the government. His first case was a minor argument involving a Texas woman, Ethel Mae Yazell, who claimed the government was wrongfully trying to force her to repay a government small business loan because the loan was taken out by her husband. Thurgood's arguments took only 18 minutes. The court ruled

in favor of Yazell. His next series of cases were very high profile. One involved the murders of three young civil rights workers, 21-year-old James Chaney from Mississippi, 24-year-old Michael Schwerner from New York, and 20-year-old Andrew Goodman from New York. The events of the case inspired the movie *Mississippi Burning*. The three were working to register black voters in Mississippi as part of Freedom Summer in 1964 and were investigating the burning of a black church. Freedom Summer was a project organized by the Council of Federated Organizations (COFO), a coalition of the Mississippi branches of the four major civil rights organizations (the Student Nonviolent Coordinating Committee (SNCC), Congress of Racial Equality (CORE), NAACP, and Southern Christian Leadership Conference (SCLC)). Because blacks in Mississippi had historically been prevented to vote, COFO's goal was to help as many as they could to register. Chaney, Schwerner, and Goodman were arrested by the police on false charges, held for several hours, and then released after dark by the Nashoba, Mississippi police department so that the three could be killed by members of the Ku Klux Klan.

The Department of Justice intervened in prosecuting those responsible because it was known they would not be charged if the case was left up to the local courts in Mississippi. However, Supreme Court intervention was required because the Court had ruled in *United States v. Cruikshank*, 92 U.S. 542 (1876) that the due process and Equal Protection Clauses only applied to state action and not to the actions of individuals. The FBI arrested 18 men in October 1964, and as expected, state prosecutors refused to try the case. Segregationist and Southern federal district judge William Harold Cox ruled that only Sherriff Lawrence Rainey, Deputy Sheriff Cecil Price and a Philadelphia, Mississippi patrolman could possibly face charges but he also ruled there was lack of evidence to try them. (Cox was the judge President Kennedy had to appoint as a trade in order to get the Senate to hold confirmation hearings to appoint Thurgood to the Second Circuit Court.)

Thurgood gave oral arguments before the Supreme Court on the importance of bringing federal charges against the accused in the combined cases of *United States v. Price*, 383 U.S. 787 (1966) and *United States v. Guest*, 383 U.S. 745 (1966). The latter case involved the shooting of Lemuel Penn, an African American reserve officer,

while he was traveling through Madison County, Georgia on the way to Washington, D.C. The alleged killers were acquitted by an all-white jury.

The Supreme Court reversed the ruling of Judge Cox in ruling that private citizens were acting on behalf of the state when acting in concert with public officials, namely the law enforcement officers. The case was remanded back to the district court. Surprisingly, the judge and all-white jury convicted seven of the accused, including Price in 1967. They were convicted on federal conspiracy charges and given sentences of 3 to 10 years, but none served more than 6. Eight of the other accused were acquitted and the last three were released after mistrials. The suspected leader of the murders, Edgar Ray "Preacher" Killen, was not convicted until January 7, 2005, at the age of 80. He was charged with three counts of murder, and accused of orchestrating the killings as well as assembling a mob to kill the victims. He was sentenced to 60 years in prison.

Another case that Thurgood lost but which had sweeping consequences was *Miranda v. Arizona*, 384 U.S. 436 (1966). Ernesto Arturo Miranda was arrested by federal agents on charges of kidnapping and rape of an 18-year-old woman. Agents never told Miranda of his rights to counsel, to remain silent, or that statements he made may be used against him later. He signed a confession that included a typed statement "I do hereby swear that I make this statement voluntarily and of my own free will, with no threats, coercion, or promises of immunity, and with full knowledge of my legal rights, understanding any statement I make may be used against me." During trial, his court-appointed lawyer, Alvin Moore, objected to the statement being used but was overruled. The case was appealed to the Arizona Supreme Court who upheld the lower court's conviction of Miranda, and finally appealed to the Supreme Court. On behalf of the government, Thurgood argued agents must have the right to interrogate witnesses and should not be limited by the need to give legal warnings or wait for victims to obtain council. In a 5–4 ruling, the Supreme Court held that confessions could not be admissible in court under the Fifth Amendment self-incrimination clause and Sixth Amendment right to an attorney unless a suspect had been made aware of their rights. The court's ruling led to the reading of Miranda Rights by law enforcement agents when

making any arrests. Although Thurgood lost the case, it showed his dedication to his position in representing the interests of the government in all legal cases.

Being loyal to federal government issues wasn't always simple for Thurgood. His obligations as solicitor general also put him a position in which he faced political turmoil that is inherent of competing interests in Washington, D.C. politics. Fred R. Black Jr., a Washington, D.C. lobbyist, was found guilty of tax evasion by the Justice Department due to evidence obtained from the FBI. However, the FBI had illegally bugged Black's hotel rooms in Washington, D.C. and Las Vegas to get the information. The Supreme Court had denied Black's appeal. Attorney General Nicholas Katzenbach felt it was the Justice Department's obligation to report the illegal bugging but realized the controversy this would cause. The FBI, under J. Edgar Hoover, would claim former Attorney General Robert Kennedy (by then a Senator) had authorized the bugging. Hoover even claimed Kennedy had listened to the taped conversations, which included conversations between Black and his attorney.

On May 24, 1966, Thurgood sent a letter to the Supreme Court revealing the bugging. In the letter, Thurgood didn't mention the Justice Department authorized the FBI to tape conversations, which infuriated Hoover. The Supreme Court reviewed Black's case and acquitted him of tax evasion. Thurgood's action protected both Kennedy and Hoover because neither were implicated.

Chapter 6

U.S. SUPREME COURT JUSTICE

In 1965, there was a vacancy on the U.S. Supreme Court and President Lyndon Johnson pondered appointing Thurgood, but decided that it was not the right time to nominate him. He felt Thurgood still needed more experience. Thurgood remained busy with both national and international legal matters as solicitor general.

In 1967, Johnson began looking for a replacement for Associate Justice Tom C. Clark. Clark retired on June 12, 1967, to avoid a conflict of interest when his son, Ramsey Clark, was appointed attorney general. President Johnson actually appointed Ramsey to force his father from the Supreme Court. Before Johnson publicly announced a nominee, there was much speculation about who he would choose for the coveted post. Johnson conferred with a number of individuals to ensure that he was selecting the right individual. When he talked with Attorney General Ramsey Clark about the possibility of appointing Thurgood, Clark surmised that Thurgood was not a traditional choice. He felt Thurgood would speak his mind, hold to his principles, and he would not succumb to political pressure from individuals or interest groups. He also felt Thurgood was a practical individual that would not only use scholarly intellect in deciding cases but he would also use common

sense. He stated, "Thurgood doesn't fit the mold. He's not a Yale man and that kind of stuff. He is just a big easy going, very humane type person. He doesn't change his behavior to suit people" (Mears, 2011).

While Johnson thought Thurgood would be the best appointee to the Supreme Court, he did consider some other African Americans. However, Nicholas Katzenbach told Johnson that if he were going to nominate an African American he should nominate Thurgood because of all of the good work he had done for the African American community and the United States. Katzenbach believed that African Americans saw Thurgood as a role model and an acceptable choice the African American community would approve of. Katzenbach confided, "Mr. President if you are going to appoint anybody, any black to that court but Thurgood Marshall, you are insulting every black. Thurgood Marshall is 'the' black lawyer in the country as far as blacks are concerned" (Williams, 1998, p. 8).

Thurgood didn't think he would receive the Supreme Court nomination. There continued to be speculation in the national media, political circles, and the Washington D.C. rumor mill on who the president would appoint. As the news of the possible selection of Thurgood circulated, critics emerged. For example, columnist David Lawrence of U.S. News and World Report published an article critical of the idea of appointing him to the Supreme Court.

President Johnson summoned Thurgood to the oval office and informed him that he would indeed be his nominee to the Supreme Court. Usually never at a loss for words, a jubilant but stunned Thurgood could only reply, "Oh, yipe!" During the conversation, Johnson explained that he wanted to appoint Thurgood as the first African American Supreme Court justice because of historical racism in the nation.

During an interview with T.H. Baker on July 10, 1969, Thurgood gave a full account of his meeting with Johnson (Smith, 2003, pp. 205–206):

Let me tell you about my appointment to the Supreme Court. I was sitting in my office, and it was about, I guess, ten o'clock in the morning. Ramsey Clark called Mrs. Lavery, who is the same secretary I have with me now, and said, "Is the Judge in?" She said,

"Yes." "Well, tell him I'm on my way." He was right there in that same hall on the fifth floor. He came on down and shut the door. He said, "What are you up to this morning?" I said, "Well, I've got to go up to the White House and talk to some students, one of these student groups, I've forgotten what it was, maybe with the Fellows, I don't know, over in the Executive Building." He said, "What time are you due up there?" I said, "Eleven o'clock." He said, "You got a car?" I said, "Well, I know Mrs. Lavery well enough to be sure she's called for a car, and there'll be a car down there waiting for me." He said, "Well, instead of getting there at eleven, you get there at a quarter of eleven. Instead of going over across the street, you go in the main. The boss wants to see you." I said, "About what?" He said, "I don't know." Ramsey, I mean, he won't tell you anything about anybody anyhow. I kept trying. He said, "I actually don't know." So I said, "Well, which way shall I go in?" There are three different ways you can go in without being seen. And he told me which way to go, and I went up there and went in and waited a few minutes. Marvin Watson came out and said, "Come on." And I went in and we chatted, the President and I. He said, "You know something, Thurgood, I'm going to put you on the Supreme Court." I said, "Well, thank you, sir." We talked a little while. We went out to the press and he announced it. We came back in the room and I said, "Now, Mr. President, if it's all right with you I'd like to call my wife. It would be better than for her to hear it on the radio." He said, "You mean you haven't called Cissy yet?" I said, "No, how could I? I've been talking to you?" So we got her on the phone and I told her to sit down. She said, "Well, I'm standing." I said, "Well, sit down." She sat down and he said, "Cissy, Lyndon Johnson." She said, "Yes, Mr. President." "I've just put your husband on the Supreme Court." She said, "I'm sure glad I'm sitting down."

Thurgood was officially nominated to the U.S. Supreme Court on June 13, 1967. During a news conference in the rose garden of the White House, Johnson stated, "I believe that this is the right thing to do, the right time to do it, the right man, and the right place" (*Time* magazine, 1967). While many celebrated the nomination of the first

African American to the Supreme Court, many others felt Thurgood's appointment was politically motivated as an astute maneuver to get African Americans to vote Democratic in the 1968 presidential election. Critics began to search for information that might derail his confirmation, led by West Virginia Senator Robert Byrd and South Carolina Senator Strom Thurmond. The two held the confirmation hearing for two months and at the same time urged J. Edgar Hoover to check Thurgood's background and social affiliations to see if he had any connections to communist governments and organizations. Byrd and Thurmond also inquired about Thurgood's involvement with the NAACP and they became increasingly and openly hostile toward Thurgood during the confirmation process, attempting to publicly humiliate him. Thurmond was a long-time opponent of Thurgood. In 1956, Thurmond was the key author of the *Southern Manifesto*, a document that was drafted and signed by Southern legislators and politicians to show their resistance to Supreme Court's ending of public school segregation in *Brown v. Board of Education of Topeka*, 347 U.S. 483 (1954).

During the confirmation hearing, Thurmond attempted to make Thurgood look incompetent through posing a series of irrelevant questions. Thurmond asked over 60 questions about legal matters pertaining to the Thirteenth, Fourteenth, and Fifteenth Amendments, which he thought would anger Thurgood publicly because these amendments deal directly with the rights of African Americans. Thurmond asked Thurgood if he knew the names of the members of the committee that drafted the Fourteenth Amendment. Thurgood responded that he did not and Thurmond then referred to Thurgood as "the stupid guy" (Kutler, 2010). Upset by Thurmond's degrading comment directed at Thurgood, Massachusetts Senator Ted Kennedy asked Thurmond if he knew the names of members of the committee that drafted the amendment, and Thurmond could not name them either. Thurmond and Byrd then took aim at what they called Thurgood's "activist legal outlook" which they argued disqualified him from becoming a member of the Supreme Court. Northern senators came to Thurgood's defense. For example, Michigan Senator Philip Hart stated, "There has never been a Supreme Court nominee whose qualifications were so dramatically and compellingly established" (*Time* magazine, 1967).

Thurgood's nomination to the Supreme Court put Southern Demo-crats in a difficult situation. If they voted in favor of his appointment, segregationists in their home states would likely stop giving them fi-nancial support and even vote them out of office. If they voted against Thurgood, they faced the possibility of losing support from the presi-dent who was also a Southerner. They would also face losing major-ity Congressional support for projects in their home states. To get Thurgood confirmed, President Johnson convinced about 20 Southern Democrats to abstain from voting. There were still 11 senators who voted against Thurgood's confirmation. All of the senators who cast "no" votes were unapologetic segregationists and all of them had par-ticipated in some form of white resistance to desegregation orders from the Supreme Court. Among them was James Eastland of Mississippi, who told President Johnson that the murder of Andrew Goodman, Mi-chael Schwerner, and James Chaney, three young civil rights activists killed in Mississippi in 1964, was a hoax and a publicity stunt. The three had been murdered by white supremacists. Congressmen Allen Ellender and Russell Long of Louisiana had once led a filibuster against a bill that would have outlawed lynching. Sam Ervin of North Carolina voted against every piece of civil rights legislation that was ever put before him. Lister Hill and John Sparkman of Alabama were signers of the *Southern Manifesto* and they voted against more than 100 potential civil rights bills (*Time* magazine, 1965). Spessard Holland of Florida and Herman Talmadge of Georgia were also signers of the *Southern Manifesto*. Talmadge declared after the *Brown* decision that "blood would run down the streets of Atlanta" (Brown-Nagin, 2011).

Despite the attempts to block Thurgood's appointment, he was confirmed by the Senate on August 30, 1967 after a vote of 69 to 11. Two days later, Associate Justice Hugo Black swore in the 59-year-old Thurgood during a private ceremony. At the ceremony, a thankful and gracious Thurgood stated, "Let me take this opportunity to reaffirm my deep faith in this nation and I pledge that I shall ever be mindful of my obligation to the Constitution and the goal of equal justice under the law" (*Time* magazine, 1967). The ceremony was the beginning of Thur-good's 24 years of service on the Supreme Court. Johnson predicted that a lot of black baby boys would thereafter be named Thurgood. Dr. Martin Luther King Jr. sent Thurgood a telegram stating, "May I

congratulate you for being appointed to the United States Supreme Court. Your appointment represents a momentous step toward a color blind society. You have proved to be a giant of your profession and your career has been one of the significant epochs of our time. You are eminently qualified and superbly equipped to serve as a Justice of the highest Court of our land" (King, 1967).

The appointment of Thurgood was one of the issues that did hurt Johnson politically. Although Johnson cited the country's schism over the Vietnam War as the reason he did not seek reelection 1968, he later admitted to Thurgood that his nomination to the Supreme Court coupled with the appointments of other African Americans to high profile positions also harmed his chances of being reelected.

Thurgood, Cecilia, and their two sons moved to Fairfax County, Virginia. Their new home was located in Lake Barcroft in the Mason District. Thurgood moved there at the invitation of Attorney General Ramsey Clark to "come integrate the community." At that time, Fairfax County had approximately 445,000 residents of which only 6.8 percent were minorities. The Marshalls were welcomed by their neighbors and invited to parties and other community functions. Cecilia later said that she had a wonderful life living in Mason District and her neighbors were just like family.

President Lyndon B. Johnson signs the Civil Rights Act on April 11, 1968. Thurgood Marshall stands to Johnson's right. (Library of Congress.)

In his new position, Thurgood was less formal with law clerks than other justices of the Supreme Court. He rarely praised his clerks, but they knew that he cared about them and their careers. He did not make them refer to him as Justice Marshall, so most of them simply called him Judge. Thurgood was meticulous in regards to his legal work. This keenness for high-quality work stemmed from when he overheard a white court official say to an attorney that he could always tell when he received a brief prepared by an African American who was poorly trained because of the misspelled words. As a result of this incident, Thurgood vowed that he or no one associated with him would ever have their work disregarded because of the sloppiness of the work. He had high expectations and made it perfectly clear that he expected work to be done well and on time. He also exercised collective discipline. When one of his law clerks did not meet his standard, Thurgood often disciplined the entire group. He knew this type of discipline would make them build a team approach to preparing cases and weed out selfish individuals.

During Thurgood's early years on the court under Chief Justice Earl Warren, he was a part of the liberal majority. However, he had a good working relationship with all the other justices because of his humorous nature. For example, his customary morning greeting to Chief Justice Warren E. Burger was "What's shaking, chiefy baby?" (Davis and Clark, 1992). Some believed that Thurgood was too closely aligned with Justice William J. Brennan Jr. President Dwight D. Eisenhower had appointed Brennan in 1956 and he served on the Court until 1990. Brennan was Thurgood's closest friend and ally on the court, and Brennan became known as the leader of the judicial liberal wing of the court. The strength of their friendship was shown when Thurgood's son named his son after both Thurgood and Brennan, Thurgood William Marshall. Brennan and Thurgood shared similar views on race and social policy. They both also supported very controversial issues such as a woman's right to have an abortion and not enforcing the death penalty. The two shared opinions in cases dealing with civil liberties, criminal justice, and civil rights, and they could each count on the other for support.

Criticism of Thurgood's appointment to the Supreme Court did not end after he became a Justice. There were continual efforts to get him

to resign. In 1970 when he was in Bethesda Naval Hospital suffering from pneumonia, a doctor walked into his room one afternoon and informed him that President Richard Nixon had asked for his medical reports. The president apparently wanted to see how close Thurgood was to death and thus how close the Republicans were to being able to name a conservative successor. Thurgood told the doctor he could send the medical records to Nixon but with the stipulation that only four words be written on the outside of the folder. The doctor agreed. Thurgood wrote on the folder in large black script: "NOT YET! DAMN IT!" (Williams, 1998, p. 348).

During Jimmy Carter's presidency, a representative of the Carter administration telephoned Thurgood and asked if he would step down so that President Carter could make a replacement Supreme Court appointment. Carter's aide reminded Thurgood of his bout of pneumonia, heart attack, and blood clots. They also warned Thurgood that if something happened to him after Carter left office, a future Republican president could appoint a conservative Justice. In anger, Thurgood slammed down the telephone and abruptly ended the conversation.

Thurgood was upset over the constant attempts to get him to resign, and deeply hurt by Democrats that supported him stepping down. He publicly stated that the appointment to the Supreme Court was a lifetime appointment and he planned to serve it in its entirety. This did not end the calls for his resignation. There was even a false news report of his death. His wife, Cecilia, was called to verify the radio report. Thurgood was in the dining room having dinner when she received the call.

Thurgood was often at odds with the more conservative majority of the Supreme Court during the 1970s and 1980s. By then Warren and other liberals left. Thurgood continued to support civil liberties, human rights, and affirmative action, and was against the death penalty. His stance on these issues was exemplified in his rulings on the following cases.

STANLEY V. GEORGIA, 349 U.S. 557 (1969)

In 1969, Thurgood wrote the majority opinion in *Stanley v. Georgia*. The case involved police using a warrant to search the home of Rob-

ert Eli Stanley's looking for betting equipment. During the search, the police found three reels of pornographic material from a desk drawer in Stanley's bedroom and charged him with possession of obscene material. Stanley was convicted and, on appeal, Georgia's Supreme Court upheld the decision. When the case came before the Supreme Court, the majority held that Stanley's First and Fourteenth Amendments has been violated and overturned the state court's decision. In his majority opinion, Thurgood noted that the right to receive information and to personal privacy were fundamental to a free society. He noted that "fundamental is the right to be free, except in very limited circumstances, from unwanted governmental intrusions into one's privacy." Thurgood believed that individuals have the "right to satisfy their intellectual and emotional needs in the privacy of his own home." Thurgood also asserted, "If the First Amendment means anything, it means that a state has no business telling a man, sitting alone in his own house, what books he may read or what films he may watch."

FURMAN V. GEORGIA, 408 U.S. 238 (1972)

William Henry Furman was burglarizing a private home in Georgia and a family member discovered him. While attempting to flee the scene, Furman tripped and fell. In doing so, the gun that Furman was carrying went off and killed one of the residents of the home. He was subsequently convicted of murder and given the death penalty. A jury convicted Furman without being providing any guidelines on how they should reach a verdict. In a 5–4 decision, the Supreme Court ruled that the death penalty was cruel and unusual punishment, which violated the Eighth Amendment of the Constitution. Thurgood delivered the majority opinion of the court, with this being the first time the Supreme Court ruled against capital punishment. In delivering the court's majority opinion, Thurgood wrote,

The death penalty is inherently unconstitutional. At a time in our history when the streets of the nation's cities inspire fear and despair, rather than pride and hope, it is difficult to maintain objectivity and concern for our fellow citizens. But the measure of a country's greatness is its ability to retain compassion in the time

of crisis. Only in a free nation could right triumph in difficult times and could civilization record its magnificent advancement. In recognizing the humanity of our fellow human beings, we pay ourselves the highest tribute. We achieve a major milestone in the long road up from barbarism and join approximately seventy other jurisdictions in the world which celebrate their regard for civilization and humanity by shunning capital punishment.

As a result of this decision, guidelines for juries were developed for death penalty cases because Thurgood and Justice Brennan also pointed out the death penalty was often used in a capricious manner that discriminated against minorities. The court reversed its position on the death penalty in *Gregg v. Georgia, Proffitt v. Florida, Jurek v. Texas, Woodson v. North Carolina,* and *Roberts v. Louisiana,* 428 U.S. 153 (1976), and upheld state statutes on its use. In essence, the court ruled its use was no longer seen as cruel and unusual punishment. Justice Potter Stewart stated that the death penalty was "cruel and unusual in the same way that being struck by lightning is cruel and unusual." He further stated, "Capital punishment is an expression of society's moral outrage at particularly offensive conduct. This function may be unappealing to many, but it is essential in an ordered society that asks its citizens to rely on legal processes rather than self-help to vindicate their wrongs." In that case and all those to follow on the issue, Thurgood dissented.

ROE V. WADE, 410 U.S. 113 (1973)

One of the most controversial Supreme Court cases in U.S. history, *Roe v. Wade,* was decided on January 22, 1973. The case involved Jane Roe (whose real name was Norma McCorvey), a single woman who wanted to abort her pregnancy. The state of Texas did not allow abortions except in the cases where the health of the mother was in jeopardy or in the case of rape. Roe filed suit against Henry Wade, the Dallas County District Attorney, claiming that her right to an abortion "performed by a competent, licensed, physician, under safe clinical conditions" was protected under the Fourteenth and Ninth Amendments of the Constitution of the United States. In a 7–2 vote the Supreme Court upheld the

lower court's decision that a Texas statute criminalizing abortion in most instances violated a woman's constitutional right of privacy. The court ruled that the Ninth Amendment, in stating that "the enumeration in the Constitution, of certain rights, shall not be construed to deny or disparage others retained by the people," protected a person's right to privacy. Justice Harry Blackmun was chosen to write the majority opinion. Blackmun found it difficult to write the opinion, particularly in finding wording that balanced the issue of women's rights and government interest in protecting health and preserving the potential life of an unborn child during the later months of pregnancy. Blackmun said in a memo to the other justices that he believed abortions should not be allowed beyond the first trimester, or the first 13 weeks, of pregnancy. Thurgood appeared concerned that this gave the states too much control after the first trimester. He expressed these sentiments in a memo to Blackmun:

Dear Harry:

I am inclined to agree that drawing the line at viability accommodates the interest at stake better than drawing it at the end of the first trimester. Given the difficulties which many women may have in believing that they are pregnant and in deciding to seek an abortion, I fear that the earlier date may not in practice serve the interest of those women, which your opinion does seek to serve. At the same time, however, I share your concern for recognizing the State's interest in insuring that abortions be done under safe conditions. If the opinion stated explicitly that, between the end of the first trimester and viability, state regulations directed at health and safely alone were permissible, I believe that those concerns would be adequately met. (Woodward, 1989)

As a result of this memo, Blackmun changed the wording of the opinion to accommodate Thurgood's concerns. Blackmun's revision includes the phrase, "that after approximately the first trimester" the states could regulate abortion to protect the health of the mother.

MILLIKEN V. BRADLEY, 418 U.S. 717 (1974)

In 1970, parents along with the Detroit Branch of the NAACP filed a class action suit against the Detroit, Michigan school system. The

suit alleged that the Detroit school system was racially segregated as a result of policy that allowed students to be bused to suburban school districts. After reviewing the case, the District Court ruled that the Detroit Board of Education submit desegregation plans for the Detroit-area schools. The federal court also ordered the state to submit desegregation plans. Subsequently, the District Court found that the plans submitted by the Detroit Board of Education were inadequate to accomplish desegregation. This was the first case on school desegregation that came before the Supreme Court since *Brown v. Board of Education*. However, the ruling in Milliken was much different. The court found that the city of Detroit had no obligation or responsibility of ensuring integration in its separate suburban school districts. As would be the case in many future cases involving segregation and civil rights, Thurgood was in dissent. He was very stern in writing his opinion:

> Desegregation is not and was never expected to be an easy task. Racial attitudes ingrained in our nation's childhood and adolescence are not quickly thrown aside in its middle years. But just as inconvenience of some cannot be allowed to stand in the way of the rights of others, so public opposition, no matter how strident, cannot be permitted to divert this court from the enforcement of the constitutional principles at issues in this case. Today's holding, I fear, is more a reflection of a perceived public mood that we have gone far enough in enforcing the Constitution's guarantee of equal justice than it is the product of neutral principles of law. In the short run, it may seem to be the easier course to allow our great metropolitan areas to be divided up each into cities—one white and the other black—but it is a course, I predict, our people will ultimately regret. I dissent.

SAN ANTONIO SCHOOL DISTRICT V. RODRIGUEZ, 411 U.S. 1 (1973)

Thurgood is remembered for his expressive dissents while serving the Supreme Court. One of his best known dissents was a 63-page opinion in the *San Antonio School District v. Rodriguez*. The majority of the court, by a 5–4 vote, held that the Constitution's guarantee of equal

protection was not violated by a property tax system used by Texas and most other states to finance public education. Under the system, districts with generous tax bases could afford to provide better schools than those that were less wealthy. In his dissenting opinion, Thurgood accused the majority of an "unsupportable acquiescence in a system which deprives children in their earliest years of the chance to reach their full potential as citizens." He argued that the right to an education should be regarded as a constitutional right, and that state policies that have the effect of discriminating on the basis of wealth should be subject to judicial scrutiny. In his dissent he wrote, "The right of every American to an equal start in life, so far as the provision of a state service as important as education is concerned, is far too vital to permit state discrimination on grounds as tenuous as those presented by this record." He criticized the rigidity of two-tiered equal protection analysis in which classifications based on race and other suspect categories were subjected to strict scrutiny while all other classifications had to be merely rational. Thurgood proposed a more flexible, sliding scale theory under which courts would examine the nature of a group being discriminated against in terms of the extent to which it had previously been subjected to discrimination, and the importance of the interests affected by legislation. Although the court did not adopt Thurgood's theory, his consistent criticism seems to have prodded the other Justices to exercise greater judicial flexibility.

REGENTS OF THE UNIVERSITY OF CALIFORNIA V. BAKKE, 438 U.S. 265 (1978)

Thurgood's dissent in *Regents of the University of California v. Bakke* exemplified his continual efforts to fight for civil rights while the majority of the Court was conservative. Allan Bakke, a 35-year-old white man, had applied to the University of California at Davis Medical School and he was denied admission twice. However, the university maintained 16 slots reserved for minorities due to its affirmative action program in order to redress longstanding and unfair exclusions of blacks from the medical profession. Bakke filed suit and claimed that he was a victim of reverse discrimination because the university admitted minorities who were less qualified than he and only because of their race.

Bakke's college grade point average and test scores were higher than those of any minority students admitted in the two years Bakke was rejected. The court's majority ruling was that race could be one of the factors considered in choosing a diverse student body in university admissions' decisions but it could not be the lone factor. More than eight months passed before the Supreme Court delivered its decision. The court was sharply divided over the affirmative action issue. Two majority opinions were presented. Each of the opinions was agreed to by a different grouping of five Justices. Justice Lewis F. Powell was central to the *Bakke* decision, being the only justice in both majorities. The two 5–4 majority opinions were delivered by Justice Powell:

1. The special admissions program with a fixed quota or number of places available only to minorities violated Title VI of the Civil Rights Act of 1964. Those places were denied to white applicants based only on their race. The university's policy was struck down and the university was ordered to admit Bakke.
2. Admissions programs do not violate the Equal Protection Clause of the Fourteenth Amendment if they consider race as one of several factors used to decide admission. Therefore, race may be considered but it may not be the only factor considered.

The *Bakke* decision angered Thurgood and led to one of his most famous dissents. He wrote,

It must be remembered that during most of the past 200 years the Constitution as interpreted by this court did not prohibit the most ingenious and pervasive forms of discrimination against the Negro. Now, when a state acts to remedy the effects of that legacy of discrimination, I cannot believe that this same Constitution stands as a barrier. . . . At every point from birth to death the impact of the past is reflected in the still disfavored position of the Negro. In light of the sorry history of discrimination and its devastating impact on the lives of Negroes, bringing the Negro into the mainstream of American life should be a state interest of the highest order. . . . The position of the Negro today in America is the tragic but inevitable (unavoidable) consequence of centuries

of unequal treatment. Measured by any benchmark of comfort or achievement, meaningful equality remains a distant dream for the Negro. . . . Now, we have the Court again stepping in, this time to stop affirmative action programs of the type used by the University of California. (*Regents of the University of California v. Bakke*, 438 U.S. 265, (1978))

The *Bakke* case began the legal dismantling of the use of affirmative action programs in higher education. In the years that followed, affirmative action was ended by state referendums and other court actions. Thurgood was disappointed that he was not able to convince the other justices to support affirmative action. He stated that the members of the court could not relate to the experiences of African Americans and the historical discrimination they experienced. He also believed that the conservative court under Chief Justice William Rehnquist was reversing many of the gains that had been won on civil rights.

Thurgood also blamed President Ronald Reagan for the reversal on civil rights during the 1980s and referred to Reagan as the "worst president on the issue of civil rights." Under Reagan and President George H. W. Bush, the Supreme Court became very conservative. Thurgood described their years in office as a step back to the days when "we [African Americans] didn't really have a chance." In a 1987 interview for *Ebony* magazine, Thurgood ranked Reagan as "the bottom" in terms of presidents who supported African Americans. Asked if he would have accepted a Supreme Court appointment if nominated by Reagan, Thurgood replied, "I wouldn't do the job of a dogcatcher for Ronald Reagan" (Williams, 1990, p. 74). He also condemned Presidents Franklin D. Roosevelt and Dwight D. Eisenhower for their poor civil rights records, and particularly Eisenhower for trying to block the Supreme Court decision in *Brown v. Board of Education of Topeka*. He praised President Johnson for his "just unbelievable" civil rights agenda. Beyond being troubled by the state of the conservative court, Thurgood faced personal grief in 1990 when Justice Brennan retired from the court for health reasons.

During Thurgood's last years serving on the court, the views of the justices continue to become more conservative. Thurgood joined the court with Earl Warren serving as chief justice. Warren was appointed

by President Dwight D. Eisenhower during a recess appointment in September 1953 and confirmed by the Senate on March 1, 1954. He was more liberal in his decisions than expected and also a skillful leader as chief justice. He was known as the "Superchief" of the Supreme Court, but so liberal that signs declaring "Impeach Earl Warren" were seen around the country during the 1960s. The court was also comprised mostly of liberal judges, due to several presidential appointments. All of the justices on the court when Warren became chief justice had been appointed by Presidents Franklin D. Roosevelt or President Harry S. Truman and were New Deal liberals, including Hugo L. Black (appointed by President Roosevelt in 1937) and William J. Brennan Jr. (appointed by President Eisenhower in 1956). Beyond the ruling in *Brown v. Board of Education* that ended segregated schools, the Warren Court ended the over-representation of rural areas in state legislatures (*Baker v. Carr*, 369 U.S. 186 (1962) and *Reynolds v. Sims*, 377 U.S. 553 (1964)), established publicly funded counsels for criminal defendants (*Gideon v. Wainwright*, 372 U.S. 335 (1963)), established the Miranda warning whereby criminals were read their rights upon arrest (*Miranda v. Arizona*, 384 U.S. 436 (1966)), and ruled against mandatory school prayer (*Engel v. Vitale*, 370 U.S. 421 (1962)). The court remained liberal with the appointment of Arthur Goldberg by President John F. Kennedy in 1962 and Thurgood in 1963.

William E. Burger was appointed chief justice in 1969 by President Richard Nixon. Burger was seen as conservative and a critic of Chief Justice Warren. It was hoped that Burger would reverse many of the liberal rulings of the court. Instead, the court upheld and even extended some liberal rulings made under Warren. The court supported busing to reduce segregation in *Swann v. Charlotte-Mecklenburg Board of Education*, 402 U.S. 1 (1971), supported abortion in *Roe v. Wade*, and supported the need for search warrants in cases of domestic surveillance in *United States v. U.S. District Court*, 407 U.S. 297 (1972). However, Burger opposed gay rights, supported the death penalty, and had strong views on punishing criminals. However, he was a weak chief justice. He upset his fellow justices by often changing his mind on cases and dedicated more of his time working on the legal system.

Harry Blackmun was appointed to the Burger Court by President Nixon in 1970 and was a lifelong Republican. At the start of his term,

he voted with Burger the majority of the time, but became liberal by the end of his term. Lewis F. Powell Jr. was appointed by President Nixon in 1972 and remained a moderate, often forging compromises between the conservative and liberal members of the court.

William Rehnquist was appointed by President Nixon in 1972 and became chief justice in 1986 under President Reagan. He was very conservative. He strongly believed in the concept of federalism and the rights of the state and local governments to be free of federal intervention under the Tenth Amendment. Thurgood, on the other hand, strongly support the rights of the federal government over that of the states. Rehnquist opposed abortion in *Roe v. Wade*, rejected the notion that the Fourteenth Amendment applied to equal rights beyond ending slavery, defended school prayer, opposed further desegregation of schools, and supported capital punishment. After Rehnquist, republican Presidents Ford, Reagan, and Bush made six appointments that changed the ideology of the court: John Paul Stevens (1975), Sandra Day O'Conner (1981), Antonin Scalia (1986), Anthony Kennedy (1988), and David Souter (1990).

Although his liberal views put him in the minority on most cases on the conservative court, Thurgood continued to support civil rights, women's rights, civil liberties, and the rights of the poor. He championed the same causes that had gotten him appointed to the court by President Johnson. For example, Thurgood had always been an advocate for poor Americans. This position was one that had been historically shared by other members of the Supreme Court appointed as New Deal judges. The court ruled in favor of government programs that provided public assistance because these programs were seen as catalysts that would help the poor become integrated into mainstream society. In *Golberg v. Kelly*, 397 U.S. 254 (1970), Justice Brennan noted that, "forces not within the control to the poor contribute to their poverty . . . welfare, by meeting the basis demands of subsistence, can help bring within the reach of the poor the same opportunities that are available of others to participate meaningfully in the life of the community." As the court became more conservative, its majority support for the poor exemplified their stance on most social issues. This was but just one area where Thurgood was in disagreement and why he became known as the "Great Dissenter." In *Dandridge v. Williams*, 397 U.S. 471

(1970), the court ruled in favor of a Maryland welfare cap of $250 to all families regardless of size. The court held their program was not in violation of the Equal Protection Clause of the Fourteenth Amendment, as the plaintiffs sought to show, because the state was trying to issue benefits to families as best as their appropriations would allow. Thurgood and Justice Brennan dissented.

Thurgood was critical of his colleagues for the majority ruling in *United States v. Kras*, 409 U.S. 434 (1973), in which the court upheld the constitutionality of a required $50 bankruptcy filing fee. The plaintiff, Robert Williams Kras, was unemployed and trying to take care of his children. One child had cystic fibrosis. In their majority ruling, the justices noted that weekly installments to pay the fee amounted to "less than the price of a movie and a little more than the cost of a pack or two of cigarettes." In his dissent, Thurgood stated,

> I cannot agree with the majority that it is so easy for the desperately poor to save $1.92 each week over the course of six months. The 1970 Census found that over 800,000 families in the Nation had annual incomes of less than $1,000, or $19.23 a week. I see

Thurgood Marshall (pictured here in 1976), the first African American appointed to the U.S. Supreme Court, built a remarkable legal career on the premise that all forms of racial segregation were unconstitutional. (Joseph Lavenburg, National Geographic Society, Collection of the Supreme Court of the United States.)

no reason to require that families in such straits sacrifice over 5% of their annual income as a prerequisite to getting a discharge in bankruptcy. It may be easy for some people to think that weekly savings of less than $2 are no burden. But no one who has had close contact with poor people can fail to understand how close to the margin of survival many of them are. . . . A pack or two of cigarettes may be, for them, not a routine purchase but a luxury indulged in only rarely. The desperately poor almost never go to see a movie, which the majority seems to believe is an almost weekly activity. They have more important things to do with what little money they have—like attempting to provide comforts for a gravely ill child, as Kras must do.

In *Personnel Administrator of Massachusetts v. Feeney*, 442 U.S. 256 (1979), Thurgood and Brennan dissented as the majority of the court ruled in favor of a state law that gave hiring preference to veterans over nonveterans. Thurgood felt the law discriminated against women since so few had veteran status. Thurgood wrote,

In the instant case, the impact of the Massachusetts statute on women is undisputed. Any veteran with a passing grade on the civil service exam must be placed ahead of a nonveteran, regardless of their respective scores. The District Court found that, as a practical matter, this preference supplants test results as the determinant of upper level civil service appointments. Because less than 2% of the women in Massachusetts are veterans, the absolute preference formula has rendered desirable state civil service employment an almost exclusively male prerogative. . . . In practice, this exemption, coupled with the absolute preference for veterans, has created a gender-based civil service hierarchy, with women occupying low-grade clerical and secretarial jobs and men holding more responsible and remunerative positions.

In *Lyng v. Castillo*, 477 U.S. 635 (1986), the court ruled that the statutory definition of *household* for the purposes of applying for food stamps constituted family members who were related. Even though several people may have been living together for years as a family unit,

sharing food and meals, they would have to apply for benefits separately if not legally married or abiding together as a result of a parental relationship. Both Thurgood and Justice Brennan dissented. In his dissent, Brennan wrote, "I would affirm on the ground that the challenged classifications violate the Equal Protection Clause because they fail the rational basis test." Thurgood wrote,

> This case demonstrates yet again the lack of vitality in this Court's recent equal protection jurisprudence. When it moved beyond the rule that merely grouped parents and children, and, in the 1982 amendments, grouped siblings together as well, Congress interfered substantially with the desires of demonstrably separate families to remain separate families. It did so, moreover, while recognizing that distinct families living together often are genuinely separate households, and that the food stamp program should permit separate families that are not related to live together, but maintain separate households. S.Rep. No. 97-504, at 25. Congress nevertheless assumed that related families are less likely to be genuinely separate households than are unrelated families, and failed even to provide related families a chance to rebut the legislative presumption. In view of the importance to the affected families of their family life and their very survival, the Court's extreme deference to this untested assumption is simply inappropriate. I respectfully dissent.

The court continued its conservative stance one of the issues most important to Thurgood during the end of his time on Supreme Court, affirmative action. In 1986, the court held that a minority set-aside program that ensured minority-owned companies would be awarded 30 percent of Richmond, Virginia's municipal contracts was unconstitutional. In *City of Richmond v. J.A. Croson, Co.*, 488 U.S. 469 (1989), the court held that the city did not identify any need for remedial action to rectify past discrimination. Therefore, it failed the test for admissible affirmative action programs. Namely, legally supported affirmative action programs were subject to strict scrutiny to ensure they were narrowly tailored to remedy prior acts of discrimination. The plaintiffs held that the city, with a population that was 50 percent

black, had a history of not awarding contracts to minorities. Thurgood, joined by Justices Brennan and Blackmun, wrote a strong dissent that sharply criticized the court for making a decision that severely reserved its longstanding stance on race-based remedies. He wrote the following:

> It is a welcome symbol of racial progress when the former capital of the Confederacy acts forthrightly to confront the effects of racial discrimination in its midst. In my view, nothing in the Constitution can be construed to prevent Richmond, Virginia, from allocating a portion of its contracting dollars for businesses owned or controlled by members of minority groups.
>
> A majority of this Court holds today, however, that the Equal Protection Clause of the Fourteenth Amendment blocks Richmond's initiative. The essence of the majority's position is that Richmond has failed to catalog adequate findings to prove that past discrimination has impeded minorities from joining or participating fully in Richmond's construction contracting industry. I find deep irony in second guessing Richmond's judgment on this point. As much as any municipality in the United States, Richmond knows what racial discrimination is; a century of decisions by this and other federal courts has richly documented the city's disgraceful history of public and private racial discrimination. In any event, the Richmond City Council *has* supported its determination that minorities have been wrongly excluded from local construction contracting. Its proof includes statistics showing that minority-owned businesses have received virtually no city contracting dollars and rarely if ever belonged to area trade associations; testimony by municipal officials that discrimination has been widespread in the local construction industry; and the same exhaustive and widely publicized federal studies relied on in *Fullilove*, studies which showed that pervasive discrimination in the Nation's tight-knit construction industry had operated to exclude minorities from public contracting. These are precisely the types of statistical and testimonial evidence which, until today, this Court had credited in cases approving of race-conscious measures designed to remedy past discrimination. More fundamentally,

today's decision marks a deliberate and giant step backward in this Court's affirmative-action jurisprudence. Cynical of one municipality's attempt to redress the effects of past racial discrimination in a particular industry, the majority launches a grapeshot attack on race-conscious remedies in general. The majority's unnecessary pronouncements will inevitably discourage or prevent governmental entities, particularly States and localities, from acting to rectify the scourge of past discrimination. This is the harsh reality of the majority's decision, but it is not the Constitution's command. The majority today sounds a full-scale retreat from the Court's longstanding solicitude to race-conscious remedial efforts 'directed toward deliverance of the century-old promise of equality of economic opportunity.' The new and restrictive tests it applies scuttle one city's effort to surmount its discriminatory past, and imperil those of dozens more localities. I, however, profoundly disagree with the cramped vision of the Equal Protection Clause which the majority offers today and with its application of that vision to Richmond, Virginia's, laudable set-aside plan. The battle against pernicious racial discrimination or its effects is nowhere near won. I must dissent. (*City of Richmond v. J. A. Croson Co.*, 488 U.S. 469 (1989))

While *City of Richmond v. J. A. Croson, Co.* applied to state governments, the Supreme Court expanded its strict scrutiny mandate to federal programs in *Adarand Constructors, Inc. v. Peña*, 515 U.S. 200 (1995). As a result, President Bill Clinton spoke on affirmative during a speech on July 19, 1995, just seven days after the court's ruling. He gave his support for affirmative action, and stated the practices should be mended but not ended. He further stated affirmative action programs should be supported as long as they did not create racial quotas, create preferences for unqualified individuals, lead to reverse discrimination, or continued after equal opportunity had been achieved.

As compared to others on the Supreme Court, Thurgood rarely gave speeches or lectures. When he accepted speaking engagements he did not waver in his support for affirmative action and the rights of the poor. Many of his speeches led to controversy because of his attacks on conservatives and even the Constitution. On May 8, 1981, he gave a

speech entitled "The Sword and the Robe" before the Second Circuit Judicial Conference that was a criticism of conservative Justices and politicians for their stance of limited protection for criminals. As part of his speech, he stated:

> This ideal of neutrality is particularly hard to maintain in times such as these, when our society faces major unsolved problems. Indeed, we judges are frequently criticized these days for our neutrality. For example, it is argued by some members of our society that the judiciary has not taken an active enough role in combating crime. It is urged that we as judges, should take sides, that we should stand shoulder to shoulder with the police and prosecutors. Convictions should be easier, appellate review more rapid and resort to habeas corpus—what the founders of this republic called the Great Writ—drastically curtailed. All of this frightens me, because when I was in law school, I was taught not that judges were there to see the defendant convicted and punished in every case but that they were there to see justice done in every case. *Of course* the state had to carry a heavy burden to obtain a conviction. *Of course* appellate judges would weigh each case carefully. *Of course* an individual, once convicted, could attack his sentence later. This, so I was taught, was not to coddle the guilty but to protect the innocent. I was raised in the days when the prevailing maxim was: 'It is better that a thousand guilty people go free than that one innocent person suffer unjustly.'
>
> Well, that's just what I was taught, and maybe I was taught wrong. But the suggestion that we as judges take sides frightens me for another, more fundamental reason as well. As I have said, judges are required in our system to be as neutral as they possibly can, to stand above the political questions in which the other branches of government are necessarily entangled. The Constitution established a legislative branch to make the laws and an executive branch to enforce them. Both branches are elected and are designed to respond to everchanging public concern, and problems. Indeed, as we were reminded just last November, the failure of either branch to respond to the will of the majority can quickly be remedied at the polls.

But the framers of the Constitution recognized that responsiveness to the will of the majority may, if unchecked, become a tyranny of the majority. They therefore created a third branch—the judiciary—to check the actions of the legislature and the executive. In order to fulfill this function, the judiciary was intentionally isolated from the political process and purposely spared the task of dealing with changing public concerns and problems. Article III judges are guaranteed life tenure. Similarly, their compensation cannot be decreased during their term in office—a provision, as we have recently seen, that certainly has its tangible benefits. Finally, the constitutional task we are assigned as judges is a very narrow one. We cannot make the laws, and it is not our duty to see that they are enforced. We merely interpret them through the painstaking process of adjudicating actual 'cases or controversies' that come before us.

We have seen what happens when the courts have permitted themselves to be moved by prevailing political pressures and have deferred to the mob rather than interpret the Constitution. *Dred Scott, Plessy, Korematsu,* and the trial proceedings in *Moore v. Dempsey,* come readily to mind as unfortunate examples. They are decisions of which the entire judicial community, even after all these years, should be ashamed. There have also been times when the courts have stood proudly as a bulwark against what was politically expedient but also unconstitutional. One need only recall the school desegregation cases to understand why this ability to stand above the fray is so important. . . . But when we accepted the judicial mantle, we yielded our right to advocate publicly our favored solutions for society's problems. The tools for solving these problems are in the hands of the other branches of government because that is where the Constitution has placed them. That is also where we should leave them. I therefore urge that you politely disregard any suggestion that you give up the robe for the sword. (Marshall, 1981)

While speaking on affirmative action in a 1986 speech to the Second Circuit Court, Thurgood urged Americans to

face the simple fact that there are groups in every community which are daily paying the cost of the history of American injustice. The argument against affirmative action is . . . an argument in favor of leaving that cost to lie where it falls. Our fundamental sense of fairness, particularly as it is embodied in the guarantee of equal protection under the laws, requires us to make an effort to see that those costs are shared equitably while we continue to work for the eradication of the consequences of discrimination. Otherwise, we must admit to ourselves that so long as the lingering effects of inequality are with us, the burden will be borne by those who are *least* able to pay.

On May 6, 1987, he spoke at the Annual Seminar of the San Francisco Patent and Trademark Association in Maui, Hawaii which marked the bicentennial celebration of the U.S. Constitution. In his speech, he was critical of the notion that the constitution was not open to interpretation and that the founding fathers developed the document without regard for the rights of blacks or women. He strongly believed its concepts should be interpreted by the court when making its rulings. He stated,

I do not believe that the meaning of the Constitution was forever "fixed" at the Philadelphia Convention. Nor do I find the wisdom, foresight, and sense of justice exhibited by the Framers particularly profound. To the contrary, the government they devised was defective from the start, requiring several amendments, a civil war, and momentous social transformation to attain the system of constitutional government, and its respect for the individual freedoms and human rights, we hold as fundamental today. When contemporary Americans cite "The Constitution," they invoke a concept that is vastly different from what the Framers barely began to construct two centuries ago. For a sense of the evolving nature of the Constitution we need to look no further than the first three words of the document's preamble: "We the People." When the Founding Fathers used this phrase in 1787, they did not have in mind the majority of America's citizens. "We

the People" included, in the words of the Framers, "the whole Number of free Persons." On a matter so basic as the right to vote, for example, Negro slaves were excluded, although they were counted for representational purposes at three-fifths each. Women did not gain the right to vote for over a hundred and thirty years. (Marshall, 1987)

The members of the Supreme Court were invited to attend a reenactment of the original deliberation of the founding fathers in writing the Constitution. Thurgood did not attend and said in an interview, "If you are going to do what you did two hundred years ago, somebody is going to give me short pants and a tray so I can serve coffee" (Williams, 1998, p. 382).

Thurgood was criticized for his views and declined more and more speaking engagements as a way to avoid unwarranted criticism and the partisan political analysis of the contents of his speeches. He was hurt with how some journalists and political cartoonists portrayed his work and service on the court. He was particularly upset over how he was portrayed in a book by Bob Woodward and Scott Armstrong entitled *The Brethren*, which painted Thurgood as lazy. He was accused of spending most of his time watching television, while his law clerks handled the heavy duty legal work (Woodward and Armstrong, 1979, p. 238). Though he was angered and deeply hurt by this characterization, he refused to respond to the authors' accusations or the media criticisms that followed. Thurgood simply stated, "I don't want to get down in the gutter" when asked about the book's portrayal of him. The *National Review* also ran a cartoon which depicted him as lazy and asleep in his chambers. These negative portrayals further pushed Thurgood away from the public eye. Toward the end of Thurgood's life, he was mostly withdrawn and rarely socialized outside of his wife and two sons' families. He had outlived many of his friends, especially the ones he was most close to, including civil rights leaders Roy Wilkins and Wiley Branton. He distanced himself from modern day civil rights leaders. Even though he did not agree with some of the methods and the techniques of the modern civil rights movement or its leaders, he did not publicly criticize them. When asked his opinion of the Reverend Jesse Jackson, Thurgood shook his head and finally snapped, "No comment."

Supreme Court members (1986–1988): (seated left to right) Thurgood Marshall, William Brennan, William Rehnquist, Byron White, Harry Blackmun, (standing) Sandra Day O'Connor, Lewis Powell Jr., John Paul Stevens, and Antonin Scalia. (Supreme Court Historical Society.)

THURGOOD MARSHALL AND THE VIETNAM WAR

The United States became involved in the Vietnam War with the goal of curtailing the spread of communism and as an act of national defense against the Soviet Union during the Cold War. These reasons were also the basis for American foreign policy during the 1950s through early 1970s (Bragg, 2005, p. 186). The United States gave military and logistics support to the democratic Republic of Vietnam (South Vietnam) and the Soviet Union supported the communist-led Democratic Republic of Vietnam (North Vietnam). Injuries and loss of life during the Vietnam War were enormous. The United States suffered 58,119 military soldiers being killed, 153,303 wounded, and 1,948 missing in action. Casualty figures for the Republic of Vietnam are estimated at 230,000 killed and 1,169,763 wounded. Combined, the North Vietnamese Army and the Viet Cong (Southern Vietnam communist forces also called the National Liberation Front) suffered approximately 1,100,000 killed in action and an unknown number of

wounded. It is estimated that between 2 to 4 million Vietnamese civilians were killed during the conflict (Weist, 2009, p.83).

The origin of the Vietnam War can be traced back to a conflict between France and communist Viet Minh in the Indochina War. This war was largely fought in Vietnam and the French were defeated in 1954. The war was settled by the Geneva Accords of 1954, which temporarily sectioned Vietnam at the 17th parallel and put the Viet Minh in control of the northern portion. The noncommunist southern portion of the nation was renamed the Republic of Vietnam and placed under the leadership of Prime Minister Ngo Dinh Diem. According to the Geneva Accords, this arrangement would last for two years and in 1956, national elections were to be held to decide the future of the nation. However, South Vietnam refused to hold reunification elections. By 1958, the Viet Cong began to wage war against the South Vietnamese government.

Initially, 2,000 military advisors from the United States were sent to train South Vietnam's army. In 1961, President Kennedy significantly increased the number of advisors to 16,300. Along with more advisors, more funding, weapons, and supplies were sent to South Vietnam. In 1961, President Kennedy ordered 100 Special Forces troops to assist with the efforts. In 1963, after the assassination of President Kennedy, President Johnson was sworn into office and he increased the United States's military involvement in Vietnam War. Johnson increased the number of American troops participating in the war and by 1964, over 16,000 had been sent to Vietnam (Pfiffner, 2011, p. 206). In March 1965, Marines began the United States ground participation in the war and President Johnson began air strikes on North Vietnam. In 1966, Johnson met with South Vietnamese premier Nguyen Cao Ky and his military advisors to make sure that the Vietnamese administration knew that democratization or the entire region was the goal and one of the key reasons the United States was involved in the war.

After Johnson left office, President Nixon's believed South Vietnam should take more responsibility for fighting the war and slowly began to withdraw American forces. However, he also attempted to slow the flow of supplies and communist forces to the region. In 1969, Nixon authorized the military to secretly bomb Cambodia to destroy the communists' supply routes and base camps there. This bombing was

conducted without the approval of Congress or the knowledge of the American public. The secret bombing campaign lasted for 14 months and, when it became public, caused increased opposition to the United States's involvement in Vietnam.

A number of groups opposed the country's involvement in the war and they staged protests in American cities, the nation's capital, and on college campuses. Veterans from World War I, War II, and the Korean War staged a protest rally in New York City in 1966. The Congress of Racial Equality (CORE) issued a report claiming that the American military draft placed "a heavy discriminatory burden on minority groups and the poor" (Willbanks, 2009, p. 168). The group also called for a withdrawal of all American troops from Vietnam. Protests continued during the 1970s, and antiwar student rallies that were held at Kent State University and Jackson State University turned deadly when national guardsmen killed student protestors. In a sermon delivered in 1967, Dr. Martin Luther King Jr. made his first public criticisms of American military involvement in the war and suggested five things that the United States could do to get out of Vietnam:

(1) End all bombing in North and South Vietnam, (2) Declare a unilateral cease-fire in the hope that such action would create the atmosphere for peace negotiations, (3) Take immediate steps to prevent other battlegrounds in Southeast Asia by curtailing military buildup in Thailand and our interference in Laos, (4) Realistically accept the fact that the National Liberation Front had substantial support in South Vietnam and must thereby play a role in any meaningful negotiations and any future Vietnam government, and (5) Set a date that the United States government would remove all foreign troops from Vietnam in accordance with the 1954 Geneva Agreement. (Branch, 2006, pp. 590–595)

Many protest groups filed lawsuits in hopes of getting the Supreme Court to prevent the president and Congress from further funding the war and to end the United States's continued involvement. Several young men filed lawsuits to prevent being drafted for military service.

Thurgood was supportive of American military operations in the Vietnam War, both as solicitor general and as a Supreme Court justice.

He had been equally supportive of the United States's involvement in the Korean War. He was fiercely patriotic and he saw the United States's action on these foreign soils as merely helping advance peace, justice, and democracy in other countries. Even though he opposed President Nixon, Thurgood would not publicly criticize the bombings in Cambodia. He, therefore, expressed disdain for people who he perceived attacked the United States's involvement in the war. He strongly supported President Johnson and was opposed to communism. He disliked King's criticism of President Johnson's policies, as well as criticisms by other black activists including Malcolm X, W.E.B. Du Bois, and Stokely Carmichael because he saw them as troublemakers who offered no alternative solutions. These activists argued the Vietnam War was another example of how the U.S. government supported the oppression of poor people of color.

Thurgood's support of the war continued when he was appointed to the Supreme Court. When a case involving the constitutionality of the war was petitioned before the court, Associate Justice William Douglas, considered the most antiwar justice on the Warren Court, could not convince Thurgood to vote in favor of hearing the case. From 1966 to 1973, the Supreme Court denied 26 cases from various courts of appeals that involved the war because the majority viewed it as a political issue that did not violate the Constitution.

A few cases involving specific individual complaints were heard by the court. In *Negre v. Larsen*, 394 U.S. 968 (1969), Thurgood wrote the 8 to 1 majority opinion that held that Catholics could not use their religion as a justification for avoiding military service. The case involved Louis Auguste Negre, who was drafted into the U.S. Army in 1967. The plaintiffs held that conscientious objectors like Negre should be allowed to disregard the draft. The court held that, "The conscription laws, applied to such persons as to others, are not designed to interfere with any religious ritual or practice, and do not work a penalty against any theological position. The incidental burdens felt by persons in petitioners' position are strictly justified by substantial governmental interests that relate directly to the very impacts questioned." The court's ruling was indicative of its majority position that if groups like the Roman Catholics were allowed the right to use conscientious objection status, then other groups could also claim this status

which would substantially reduce the number of people available for military service.

Other conscientious objection cases did not use religion as a reason for objection but rather race and the racial composition of the draft board. In some cases, black men challenged induction on the ground that pervasive underrepresentation of blacks in the membership of local draft boards was discriminatory. The most famous of these cases, *Clay v. United States*, 403 U.S. 698 (1971), involved heavyweight boxing champion Muhammad Ali and his refusal to be drafted into the U.S. Army. In 1966, he publicly stated he was a conscientious objector because of his religion. As a Muslim, he stated war was against the teachings of the Quran and he had no quarrel with the Viet Cong. Ali later was convicted of draft evasion and became one of the leading voices in the antiwar movement by giving speeches on college campuses criticizing the war and racism in America. As a result of his actions, the New York State Athletic Commission suspended his boxing license and stripped him of his title. Other boxing commissions did the same. Ali began a legal battle that lasted nearly five years and ended with a Supreme Court unanimous decision. The court overturned Ali's draft conviction on the grounds that the government had failed to properly specify why Ali's application had been denied. Thurgood abstained from the Ali case.

Other conscientious objection cases included *Mitchell v. United States*, 386 U.S. 972 (1967), *Luftig v. McNamara*, 387 U.S. 945 (1967), *Mora v. McNamara*, 389 U.S. 934 (1967), *Hart v. United States*, 391 U.S. 956 (1968), and *Holmes v. United States*, 391 U.S. 936 (1968).

In June 1973, Congress voted to discontinue any funding of American military activities in Cambodia starting August 15, 1973. New York Congresswoman Elizabeth Holtzman filed suit against Secretary of Defense James R. Schlesinger. On July 25, 1973, the District Court for the Eastern District of New York issued a permanent injunction prohibiting the Department of Defense from any further bombings or military actions in Cambodia. On July 27, 1973, the U.S. Court of Appeals for the Second Circuit stayed the District's Court injunction and military action continued. Holtzman and the other plaintiffs appealed to Thurgood because he was the circuit justice. In *Schlesinger v. Holtzman*, 414 U.S. 1321 (1973), Thurgood refused to order the stay.

The plaintiffs then appealed to Justice Douglas on August 4, 1973, who supported the stay order, thus stopping any further bombings. On the same day, Thurgood got support from all the other justices, allowing the bombings to continue. The court's ruling was that the Constitution placed military action under the executive and legislative branches of government, and the judicial branch, therefore, would not rule on what they saw as a political matter.

Toward the end of the Vietnam War, Thurgood's support had changed. He no longer wholeheartedly backed the war but remained fairly silent on his views. The Paris Peace Accords officially brought an end to the war. This settlement was signed on January 27, 1973. The terms of the accords called for a complete ceasefire in South Vietnam but allowed North Vietnamese forces to retain the territory they had captured. The accords also allowed American prisoners of war to be released. After the Paris Peace Accords was signed, the United States withdrew its remaining forces from the region. The Vietnam War had lasted 19 years and the United States was involved for 15 years.

Chapter 7

THE LEGACY OF THURGOOD MARSHALL

Thurgood's legacy and the recognitions of his contributions to law began years before he retired from the Supreme Court. The Thurgood Marshall College Fund (TMCF) was founded in 1987 under the leadership of Dr. N. Joyce Payne in cooperation with Miller Brewing Co., Sony Music, the National Basketball Association, Reebok, and the American Association for State Colleges and Universities. The fund is a 501(c) 3, tax-exempt organization, which provides scholarships for individuals to attend historically black colleges and universities. It represents 47 public historically black colleges and universities and their 235,000 students located in 22 states, the District of Columbia and the U.S. Virgin Islands. The mission of the fund is to partner with member schools to increase access, retention, and graduation rates of students attending their schools, identify and prepare member schools' students who have significant leadership potential, and create a pipeline of highly qualified member schools' students and alumni. The TMCF has enabled over 12,000 students to attend public historically black colleges and universities. Nationally, over 2 million young people have graduated from TMCF-member schools. Nearly one in seven Bachelor's degrees earned by African Americans was earned at TMCF member

schools and 86 percent of all students who attend a TMCF-member school rely on financial aid in their pursuit of a degree.

In early 1990, a reporter asked Thurgood about his plans for retirement from the court. Thurgood replied, "I have a lifetime appointment and I intend to serve it. I expect to die at 110, shot by a jealous husband" (Ball, 1998, p. 77). Toward the end of his career, Marshall was hard of hearing and wore two hearing aids and suffered from glaucoma. His battle with glaucoma did not cure his insatiable appetite for reading and he continued to be an avid reader. On June 27, 1991, Marshall stepped down from the Supreme Court because his health was failing. The following is the letter he sent to President George H. W. Bush on June 27, 1991:

My Dear Mr. President:

The strenuous demands of Court work and its related duties required or expected of a Justice appear at this time to be incompatible with my advancing age and medical condition.

I, therefore, retire as an Associate Justice of the Supreme Court of the United States when my successor is qualified.

Respectfully,
Thurgood Marshall (Haugen, 2007, p. 90)

In response to Thurgood's letter of resignation, President Bush wrote back on June 28, 1991:

Dear Mr. Justice:

It is with deep regret that I acknowledge your letter of retirement from the Supreme Court effective at such time as a successor is qualified.

Our Nation is deeply indebted to you for your long and distinguished public service. Your courageous leadership in the fight for equal opportunity, exemplified by your brief and oral argument in the landmark case of Brown v. Board of Education, is a powerful example of how one person's commitment to his convictions can shape a nation's attitude on such a fundamental issue.

Your distinguished service to our country, first on the U.S. Court of Appeals for the Second Circuit, as our Nation's 33rd

Solicitor General, and capped by a great career on the Supreme Court will also be long remembered.

Barbara and I wish you happiness and every blessing in your years of retirement.

Sincerely,

George Bush (Bush, 1991)

(Both letters can be found in the George Bush Presidential Library and Museum, http://bushlibrary.tamu.edu/research/public_papers.php ?id=3147&year=1991&month=6)

On the day of his retirement, Thurgood heard his last Supreme Court case. In *Payne v. Tennessee,* 501 U.S. 88 (1991), he gave one of his strongest dissents and criticisms of the court. Pervis Tyrone Payne was convicted by a Tennessee jury of the first-degree murders of Charisse Christopher and her two-year-old daughter, and of first-degree assault with intent to murder Charisse's three-year-old son Nicholas. The crimes were committed in the victims' apartment after Charisse resisted Payne's sexual advances. During the sentencing phase of the trial, state prosecutors called Payne's parents and girlfriend, and a clinical psychologist, each of whom testified as to various mitigating aspects of his background and character. They also called Nicholas's grandmother, who testified that Nicholas missed his mother and baby sister. In arguing for the death penalty, the prosecutor commented on the continuing effects on Nicholas from his experience and on the effects of the crimes upon the victims' family. The jury sentenced Payne to death on each of the murder counts. The State Supreme Court affirmed, rejecting Payne's defense contention that the admission of the grandmother's testimony violated his Eighth Amendment rights, as the Supreme Court had ruled in under *Booth v. Maryland,* 482 U.S. 496 (1987), and *South Carolina v. Gathers,* 490 U.S. 805 (1989). In both of these prior cases, the court held that evidence and argument relating to the victim and the impact of the victim's death on the victim's family were inadmissible in a capital sentencing hearing. In *Payne,* however, the court ruled that these "victim impact statements" were admissible. Thurgood was joined by Justice Blackman in his strong dissent:

Power, not reason, is the new currency of this Court's decision-making. Four Terms ago, a five-Justice majority of this Court held that "victim impact" evidence of the type at issue in this case could not constitutionally be introduced during the penalty phase of a capital trial. *Booth v. Maryland*, 482 U.S. 496 (1987). By another 5–4 vote, a majority of this Court rebuffed an attack upon this ruling just two Terms ago. *South Carolina v. Gathers*, 490 U.S. 805 (1989). Nevertheless, having expressly invited respondent to renew the attack, 498 U.S. 1076 (1991), today's majority overrules *Booth* and *Gathers* and credits the dissenting views expressed in those cases. Neither the law nor the facts supporting *Booth* and *Gathers* underwent any change in the last four years. Only the personnel of this Court did.

In dispatching *Booth* and *Gathers* to their graves, today's majority ominously suggests that an even more extensive upheaval of this Court's precedents may be in store. Renouncing this Court's historical commitment to a conception of "the judiciary as a source of impersonal and reasoned judgments," *Moragne v. States Marine Lines*, 398 U.S. 375, 398 U.S. 403 (1970), the majority declares itself free to discard any principle of constitutional liberty which was recognized or reaffirmed over the dissenting votes of four Justices and with which five or more Justices now disagree. The implications of this radical new exception to the doctrine of *stare decisis* are staggering. The majority today sends a clear signal that scores of established constitutional liberties are now ripe for reconsideration, thereby inviting the very type of open defiance of our precedents that the majority rewards in this case. Because I believe that this Court owes more to its constitutional precedents in general and to *Booth* and *Gathers* in particular. I dissent. (*South Carolina v. Gathers*, 490 U.S. 805 (1989))

Rather than with sadness, Thurgood displayed his trademark sense of humor throughout this retirement announcement. During a press conference, a reporter asked him how he was feeling. Thurgood replied, "With my hands." When another asked what was wrong with him, he replied, "What's wrong with me? I'm old. I'm getting old and coming apart" (Crowe, 2008, p. 204). During that interview, Thurgood

became very agitated when a reporter asked if he was retiring because he was tired of being part of such a conservative Supreme Court. Thurgood retorted that his feelings about the court had nothing to do with his decision, but only his failing health.

Thurgood did not believe his replacement on the court had to be African American. He believed that his replacement should be qualified. He stated that his daddy once told him, "There's no difference between a black snake and a white snake. They both bite." Marshall further stated "I think the next Justice should be a qualified person. The best person they can find, and I would hope that it would be a Negro" (Toobin, 2008, p. 30). However, he was unhappy that the next justice would be chosen by President George H. W. Bush. That would mean another conservative would be appointed and one that was most likely opposed to civil rights and other issues most important to Thurgood.

President Bush named Clarence Thomas, a 43-year-old conservative African American, as Marshall's replacement. Thomas's conservative ideology was opposite to Thurgood in many ways. Thomas opposed affirmative action, abortion, and federal interference in state governments. During his tenure on the bench, many called him the most conservative justice on the court.

In 1992, the American Bar Association established the Thurgood Marshall Award to recognize contributions by lawyers who have advanced and exemplified the commitment of Thurgood in the areas of civil rights, civil liberties, and human rights. Past recipients of the award have included Oliver W. Hill (civil rights attorney and Columbia University professor) in 1996, Stephen N. Bright (director of the Southern Center for Human Rights) in 1998, Associate Justice Ruth Bader Ginsburg in 1999, the Honorable Revius Q. Ortique Jr. (the first African American elected to the Louisiana Supreme Court) in 2000, and the Honorable Janet Reno (former U.S. attorney general) in 2009.

The Thurgood Marshall Federal Judiciary Building was completed in 1992. The building houses agencies that support the work of the U.S. Federal Courts, including the Administrative Office of the U.S. Courts, the Federal Judicial Center, and the U.S. Sentencing Commission. The building is located on One Columbus Circle Northeast Street near the U.S. Capitol in Washington D.C. and has over a half a million square feet of office space with a striking five-story atrium.

Two years after retiring, Marshall died on January 24, 1993, at the National Naval Medical Center in Bethesda, Maryland, of congestive heart failure at age 84. On January 27, 1993, his casket was placed in the Great Hall at the Supreme Court for public viewing. Approximately 20,000 people came to pay their respects to the man who was a champion for civil rights and the rights of the poor. One mourner left a copy of Marshall's brief from the *Brown v. Board of Education of Topeka* case on the casket. A memorial service was held at the Washington National Cathedral the following day. Among the 4,000 people that attended the funeral were President Bill Clinton and his wife Hillary, and Vice President Al Gore and his wife Tipper. A choir from Howard University sang hymns between the various speakers. Thurgood was remembered for his tenacity, creativity, and success achieving significant victories in the civil rights movement. In his eulogy, Chief Justice William H. Rehnquist spoke of the words inscribed above the front entrance of the Supreme Court, "Equal Justice for All," in remembering Thurgood. Rehnquist stated "Surely no one individual did more to make these words a reality than Thurgood Marshall." He also stated, "His remarkable accomplishments as a private lawyer were followed by appointment to the Court of Appeals for the Second Circuit, as solicitor general, and finally as an associate justice of the Supreme Court. In these quite different roles, his contributions to public law were necessarily of a different kind. On the Supreme Court, he continued to be a vigorous champion of civil rights for minorities and civil liberty for all; sometimes in the majority, just as often in dissent. But he authored important opinions in areas of the law quite apart from those with which he is usually associated" (Tobias, 1999, p. 108).

Thurgood was buried in a private ceremony at Arlington National cemetery and his grave site is located near the graves of fellow Supreme Court justices Oliver Wendell Holmes Jr., William O. Douglas, William J. Brennan, and Potter Stewart. Marshall was frequently asked how he would like to be remembered, and he would generally respond, "That is left up to the people." When pressed on the question he responded, "I did the best that I could with what I had" (*Ebony* magazine, 1991, pp. 110–118).

On May 10, 2010, President Barack Obama nominated Elena Kagan to become an associate justice on the Supreme Court. She was the first

solicitor general confirmed to the court since Thurgood. Kagan had previously served as a law clerk for Thurgood and she expressed her admiration for the way he approached law. However, during her confirmation hearing her support of Thurgood's legal philosophies became an issue, especially by some Republican Senators. Thurgood's name was mentioned 35 times during Kagan's confirmation hearing (Bellantoni, 2010).

Senator Jon Kyl of Arizona and Senator Jeff Session of Alabama criticized memos that Kagan sent when she was Thurgood's law clerk. They believed these memos were evidence that she would be an activist judge and politics would guide her decision making on the court. They believed that Kagan was very opinionated and she would use the law to achieve specific policy results rather than deciding legal questions and cases on their merits. These were the same concerns Southern senators had during Thurgood's appointments. Senator Kyl stated, "There's a disturbing pattern that evolves here when you read these [memos] that suggests that she is more interested in taking a case or not taking it based upon how they can advance the law to suit themselves or play defense against a court that she thinks might make bad law" (Davis, 2010). The two senators also cited notes that Kagan wrote to Marshall in which she argued that the Supreme Court should not take certain cases based on her fear that they would give its conservative majority the chance to scale back abortion and criminal rights, among others. During Senator Kyl's questioning, he criticized Thurgood's judicial philosophy by stating, "Justice Marshall's judicial philosophy, however, is not what I would consider to be mainstream. As he once explained, you do what you think is right and let the law catch up. He might be the epitome of a results-oriented judge" (Espo, 2010). Senator Jeff Session branded Marshall a "well-known activist judge" (Bellantoni, 2010). Session further criticized Kagan for having "associated herself with well-known activist judges who have used their power to redefine the meaning of our constitution and have the result of advancing that judge's preferred social policies." Senator John Cornyn of Texas stated that Marshall was a judicial activist with a judicial philosophy that concerned him. Elena Kagan was endorsed by Thurgood Marshall Jr. who referred to her as scary smart. Kagan was confirmed by a 63–37 Senate vote on August 5, 2010.

Many honors have been bestowed on Thurgood both before and since his death. During his lifetime, he received more than 20 honorary degrees from institutions in the United States and internationally. On February 14, 1976, the law school at Texas Southern University was formally named the Thurgood Marshall School of Law. He received this honor because he was the NAACP's chief counsel that argued on behalf of Heman M. Sweatt and his efforts to enroll into law school at the University of Texas during segregation. Thurgood Marshall College was founded in 1970. Originally named Third College, its name was changed by the University of California, San Diego to honor Thurgood in July 1993. In 1993, the University of Maryland renamed it law school's library after Thurgood. In 2000, the historic Twelfth Street YMCA building located in the Shaw neighborhood of Washington, D.C. was renamed the Thurgood Marshall Center. As a part of the 26th edition of its Black Heritage series, the U.S. Postal Service issued a stamp in Thurgood's honor on January 7, 2003. The stamp features a photograph of Marshall with his trademark black horn-rimmed eye glasses with a slight smile and wearing his black judicial robe. The photograph was originally taken by photographer Abdon Daoud Ackad shortly after Thurgood became a Supreme Court justice in 1967. The stamp was designed by Richard Sheaff of Scottsdale, Arizona and remains one of the most popular in the Black Heritage collection (U.S. Postal Service, 2003).

In 2003, the federal courthouse at Foley Square in Manhattan, New York was named after Thurgood. It was completed in 1995 and while constructing the building, it was discovered that the grounds had been an 18th century African American burial ground. Thurgood worked in the courthouse from 1961 to 1965. On October 1, 2005, the Baltimore–Washington International Airport was renamed Baltimore–Washington International Thurgood Marshall Airport.

In 2010, Laurence Fishburne starred in a one-man play entitled *Thurgood*. The play was written by George Stevens Jr. and was directed by Leonard Foglia. The play covers Thurgood from his early days as a young spirited civil rights lawyer through his retirement from the Supreme Court. The play received rave reviews and critical acclaim. In February 2011, the Home Box Office (HBO) channel aired a live performance of the play that was taped at the Eisenhower Theater at the

Kennedy Center in Washington, D.C. Fishburne's portrayal of Marshall was endorsed by veteran actor Sidney Poitier who played Marshall in the television movie *Separate But Equal* in 1991. Poitier also received critical acclaim for his portrayal of Thurgood, a role for which Poitier was nominated for both a Golden Globe award and an Emmy award. Speaking about Fishburne's portrayal of Thurgood, Poitier described it as "exquisite, absolutely exquisite. . . . I got to know Mr. Thurgood Marshall because I was about to play him, so I had to learn about him. I saw tonight some of the real substantive characteristics of the Thurgood Marshall that I got to know" (Lacher, 2010). Both Fishburne and Poitier acknowledged that Thurgood was a very important figure in not only African American history, but in American history.

In 2010, May 17 was declared Thurgood Marshall Day in the state of New York. The law establishing this annual day of commemoration was introduced by New York Assemblywoman Ellen Jaffee (D-Suffern) and Senator Thomas Morahan (R-New City) in honor of Thurgood's winning of a disparity case that integrated Main School, now known as the Hillburn School, in Rockland County, New York. The 1943 case resulted from black parents complaining their children in Ramapo attended the Brook School, a wood structure with no gymnasium, library, or indoor bathrooms, while white children attended Main School that had a gymnasium, library, and indoor plumbing. It was also on May 17, 1954 that the Supreme Court handed down its ruling in *Brown v. Board of Education of Topeka.*

Another part of Thurgood's legacy is that many of his law clerks later became judges themselves. These include Judge Douglas Ginsburg of the D.C. Circuit Court of Appeals, Judge Ralph Winter of the U.S. Court of Appeals for the Second Circuit, and Supreme Court Justice Elena Kagan. Others became notable law professors including Dan Kahan, Cass Sunstein, Eben Moglen, Susan Low Bloch, Martha Minow, Rick Pildes, Paul Gewirtz, and Mark Tushnet. Two others became law school deans, Paul Mahoney of the University of Virginia School of Law, and Richard Revesz of New York University School of Law.

APPENDIX

Thurgood Marshall's Eulogy Delivered by Chief Justice William H. Rehnquist Washington Cathedral, Washington, D.C., January 28, 1993

Source: Rehnquist, Chief Justice William H. "Eulogy for Thurgood Marshall." Washington Cathedral, Washington D.C., January 28, 1993.

Supreme Court Justice and civil rights advocate Thurgood Marshall was born in Baltimore, the son of William and Norma (Williams) Marshall. In 1929, he married Vivian Burey. He later married Cecilia S. Suyat in 1955. Marshall was the father of two children. He received a bachelor of arts degree from Lincoln University in 1930, and was the class of 1933's valedictorian from Howard University Law School.

Marshall practiced law in Baltimore from 1933 to 1937, and in 1938 became national counsel for the NAACP. The following year he helped found the organization's Legal Defense and Educational Fund, whose purpose was to legally challenge segregation. During this time, he won twenty-nine out of thirty-two cases he argued, the most famous being the 1954 landmark *Brown v. Board of Education*, which struck down segregation in the nation's public schools.

He was appointed U.S. Circuit Judge for the federal appeals circuit in 1961, and was Solicitor General of the United States from 1965 to 1967.

President Lyndon Johnson appointed Marshall a U.S. Supreme Court Justice in 1967, the first African American to hold the office. A consistent liberal, Marshall found himself increasingly in the minority as the makeup of the Court evolved.

Marshall retired in 1991 due to ill health, and his seat was occupied by Clarence Thomas.

"*Brown v. Board of Education of Topeka*, 347 U.S. 483 (1954)"
Appeal from the United States District Court for the District of Kansas. No. 1. Argued December 9, 1952. Reargued December 8, 1953. Decided May 17, 1954.

Source: *Brown v. Board of Education*. 347 U.S. 483 (1954).

Segregation of white and Negro children in the public schools of a State solely on the basis of race, pursuant to state laws permitting or re-quiring such segregation, denies to Negro children the equal protection of the laws guaranteed by the Fourteenth Amendment—even though the physical facilities and other "tangible" factors of white and Negro schools may be equal. Pp. 486–496.

(a) The history of the Fourteenth Amendment is inconclusive as to its intended effect on public education. Pp. 489–490.

(b) The question presented in these cases must be determined, not on the basis of conditions existing when the Fourteenth Amendment was adopted, but in the light of the full devel-opment of public education and its present place in Ameri-can life throughout the Nation. Pp. 492–493.

(c) Where a State has undertaken to provide an opportunity for an education in its public schools, such an opportunity is a right which must be made available to all on equal terms. P. 493.

(d) Segregation of children in public schools solely on the basis of race deprives children of the minority group of equal edu-cational opportunities, even though the physical facilities and other "tangible" factors may be equal. Pp. 493–494.

(e) The "separate but equal" doctrine adopted in Plessy v. Ferguson, 163 U.S. 537, has no place in the field of public education. P. 495. [347 U.S. 483, 484]

(f) The cases are restored to the docket for further argument on specified questions relating to the forms of the decrees. Pp. 495–496.

[Footnote *] Together with No. 2, Briggs et al. v. Elliott et al., on appeal from the District Court for the Eastern District of South Carolina, argued December 9–10, 1952, reargued December 7–8, 1953; No. 4, Davis et al. v. County School Board of Prince Edward County, Virginia, et al., on appeal from the United States District Court for the Eastern District of Virginia, argued December 10, 1952, reargued December 7–8, 1953; and No. 10, Gebhart et al. v. Belton et al., on certiorari to the Supreme Court of Delaware, argued December 11, 1952, reargued December 9, 1953.

Robert L. Carter argued the cause for appellants in No. 1 on the original argument and on the reargument. Thurgood Marshall argued the cause for appellants in No. 2 on the original argument and Spottswood W. Robinson, III, for appellants in No. 4 on the original argument, and both argued the causes for appellants in Nos. 2 and 4 on the reargument. Louis L. Redding and Jack Greenberg argued the cause for respondents in No. 10 on the original argument and Jack Greenberg and Thurgood Marshall on the reargument.

On the briefs were Robert L. Carter, Thurgood Marshall, Spottswood W. Robinson, III, Louis L. Redding, Jack Greenberg, George E. C. Hayes, William R. Ming, Jr., Constance Baker Motley, James M. Nabrit, Jr., Charles S. Scott, Frank D. Reeves, Harold R. Boulware and Oliver W. Hill for appellants in Nos. 1, 2 and 4 and respondents in No. 10; George M. Johnson for appellants in Nos. 1, 2 and 4; and Loren Miller for appellants in Nos. 2 and 4. Arthur D. Shores and A. T. Walden were on the Statement as to Jurisdiction and a brief opposing a Motion to Dismiss or Affirm in No. 2.

Paul E. Wilson, Assistant Attorney General of Kansas, argued the cause for appellees in No. 1 on the original argument and on the reargument. With him on the briefs was Harold R. Fatzer, Attorney General.

John W. Davis argued the cause for appellees in No. 2 on the original argument and for appellees in Nos. 2 and 4 on the reargument. With him on the briefs in No. 2 were T.C. Callison, Attorney General of South Carolina, Robert McC. Figg, Jr., S.E. Rogers, William R. Meagher and Taggart Whipple [347 U.S. 483, 485]

J. Lindsay Almond, Jr. Attorney General of Virginia, and T. Justin Moore argued the cause for appellees in No. 4 on the original argument and for appellees in Nos. 2 and 4 on the reargument. On the briefs in No. 4 were J. Lindsay Almond, Jr., Attorney General, and Henry T. Wickham, Special Assistant Attorney General, for the State of Virginia, and T. Justin Moore, Archibald G. Robertson, John W. Riely and T. Justin Moore, Jr. for the Prince Edward County School Authorities, appellees.

H. Albert Young, Attorney General of Delaware, argued the cause for petitioners in No. 10 on the original argument and on the reargument. With him on the briefs was Louis J. Finger, Special Deputy Attorney General.

By special leave of Court, Assistant Attorney General Rankin argued the cause for the United States on the reargument, as amicus curiae, urging reversal in Nos. 1, 2 and 4 and affirmance in No. 10. With him on the brief were Attorney General Brownell, Philip Elman, Leon Ulman, William J. Lamont and M. Magdelena Schoch. James P. McGranery, then Attorney General, and Philip Elman filed a brief for the United States on the original argument, as amicus curiae, urging reversal in Nos. 1, 2 and 4 and affirmance in No. 10.

Briefs of amici curiae supporting appellants in No. 1 were filed by Shad Polier, Will Maslow and Joseph B. Robison for the American Jewish Congress; by Edwin J. Lukas, Arnold Forster, Arthur Garfield Hays, Frank E. Karelsen, Leonard Haas, Saburo Kido and Theodore Leskes for the American Civil Liberties Union et al.; and by John Ligtenberg and Selma M. Borchardt for the American Federation of Teachers. Briefs of amici curiae supporting appellants in No. 1 and respondents in No. 10 were filed by Arthur J. Goldberg and Thomas E. Harris [347 U.S. 483, 486] for the Congress of Industrial Organizations and by Phineas Indritz for the American Veterans Committee, Inc.

MR. CHIEF JUSTICE WARREN delivered the opinion of the Court.

These cases come to us from the States of Kansas, South Carolina, Virginia, and Delaware. They are premised on different facts and different local conditions, but a common legal question justifies their consideration together in this consolidated opinion.[1] [347 U.S. 483, 487]

In each of the cases, minors of the Negro race, through their legal representatives, seek the aid of the courts in obtaining admission to the public schools of their community on a nonsegregated basis. In each instance, [347 U.S. 483, 488] they had been denied admission to schools attended by white children under laws requiring or permitting segregation according to race. This segregation was alleged to deprive the plaintiffs of the equal protection of the laws under the Fourteenth Amendment. In each of the cases other than the Delaware case, a three-judge federal district court denied relief to the plaintiffs on the so-called "separate but equal" doctrine announced by this Court in Plessy v. Ferguson, 163 U.S. 537. Under that doctrine, equality of treatment is accorded when the races are provided substantially equal facilities, even though these facilities be separate. In the Delaware case, the Supreme Court of Delaware adhered to that doctrine, but ordered that the plaintiffs be admitted to the white schools because of their superiority to the Negro schools.

The plaintiffs contend that segregated public schools are not "equal" and cannot be made "equal," and that hence they are deprived of the equal protection of the laws. Because of the obvious importance of the question presented, the Court took jurisdiction.[2] Argument was heard in the 1952 Term, and reargument was heard this Term on certain questions propounded by the Court.[3] [347 U.S. 483, 489]

Reargument was largely devoted to the circumstances surrounding the adoption of the Fourteenth Amendment in 1868. It covered exhaustively consideration of the Amendment in Congress, ratification by the states, then existing practices in racial segregation, and the views of proponents and opponents of the Amendment. This discussion and our own investigation convince us that, although these sources cast some light, it is not enough to resolve the problem with which we are faced. At best, they are inconclusive. The most avid proponents of the post-War Amendments undoubtedly intended them to remove all legal distinctions among "all persons born or naturalized in the United

States." Their opponents, just as certainly, were antagonistic to both the letter and the spirit of the Amendments and wished them to have the most limited effect. What others in Congress and the state legislatures had in mind cannot be determined with any degree of certainty.

An additional reason for the inconclusive nature of the Amendment's history, with respect to segregated schools, is the status of public education at that time.[4] In the South, the movement toward free common schools, supported [347 U.S. 483, 490] by general taxation, had not yet taken hold. Education of white children was largely in the hands of private groups. Education of Negroes was almost nonexistent, and practically all of the race were illiterate. In fact, any education of Negroes was forbidden by law in some states. Today, in contrast, many Negroes have achieved outstanding success in the arts and sciences as well as in the business and professional world. It is true that public school education at the time of the Amendment had advanced further in the North, but the effect of the Amendment on Northern States was generally ignored in the congressional debates. Even in the North, the conditions of public education did not approximate those existing today. The curriculum was usually rudimentary; ungraded schools were common in rural areas; the school term was but three months a year in many states; and compulsory school attendance was virtually unknown. As a consequence, it is not surprising that there should be so little in the history of the Fourteenth Amendment relating to its intended effect on public education.

In the first cases in this Court construing the Fourteenth Amendment, decided shortly after its adoption, the Court interpreted it as proscribing all state-imposed discriminations against the Negro race.[5] The doctrine of [347 U.S. 483, 491] "separate but equal" did not make its appearance in this Court until 1896 in the case of Plessy v. Ferguson, supra, involving not education but transportation.[6] American courts have since labored with the doctrine for over half a century. In this Court, there have been six cases involving the "separate but equal" doctrine in the field of public education.[7] In Cumming v. County Board of Education, 175 U.S. 528, and Gong Lum v. Rice, 275 U.S. 78, the validity of the doctrine itself was not challenged.[8] In more recent cases, all on the graduate school [347 U.S. 483, 492] level, inequality was found in that specific benefits enjoyed by white students were denied to

Negro students of the same educational qualifications. Missouri ex rel. Gaines v. Canada, 305 U.S. 337; Sipuel v. Oklahoma, 332 U.S. 631; Sweatt v. Painter, 339 U.S. 629; McLaurin v. Oklahoma State Regents, 339 U.S. 637. In none of these cases was it necessary to re-examine the doctrine to grant relief to the Negro plaintiff. And in Sweatt v. Painter, supra, the Court expressly reserved decision on the question whether Plessy v. Ferguson should be held inapplicable to public education.

In the instant cases, that question is directly presented. Here, unlike Sweatt v. Painter, there are findings below that the Negro and white schools involved have been equalized, or are being equalized, with respect to buildings, curricula, qualifications and salaries of teachers, and other "tangible" factors.[9] Our decision, therefore, cannot turn on merely a comparison of these tangible factors in the Negro and white schools involved in each of the cases. We must look instead to the effect of segregation itself on public education.

In approaching this problem, we cannot turn the clock back to 1868 when the Amendment was adopted, or even to 1896 when Plessy v. Ferguson was written. We must consider public education in the light of its full development and its present place in American life throughout [347 U.S. 483, 493] the Nation. Only in this way can it be determined if segregation in public schools deprives these plaintiffs of the equal protection of the laws.

Today, education is perhaps the most important function of state and local governments. Compulsory school attendance laws and the great expenditures for education both demonstrate our recognition of the importance of education to our democratic society. It is required in the performance of our most basic public responsibilities, even service in the armed forces. It is the very foundation of good citizenship. Today it is a principal instrument in awakening the child to cultural values, in preparing him for later professional training, and in helping him to adjust normally to his environment. In these days, it is doubtful that any child may reasonably be expected to succeed in life if he is denied the opportunity of an education. Such an opportunity, where the state has undertaken to provide it, is a right which must be made available to all on equal terms.

We come then to the question presented: Does segregation of children in public schools solely on the basis of race, even though the physical facilities and other "tangible" factors may be equal, deprive

the children of the minority group of equal educational opportunities? We believe that it does.

In Sweatt v. Painter, supra, in finding that a segregated law school for Negroes could not provide them equal educational opportunities, this Court relied in large part on "those qualities which are incapable of objective measurement but which make for greatness in a law school." In McLaurin v. Oklahoma State Regents, supra, the Court, in requiring that a Negro admitted to a white graduate school be treated like all other students, again resorted to intangible considerations: "... his ability to study, to engage in discussions and exchange views with other students, and, in general, to learn his profession" [347 U.S. 483, 494]. Such considerations apply with added force to children in grade and high schools. To separate them from others of similar age and qualifications solely because of their race generates a feeling of inferiority as to their status in the community that may affect their hearts and minds in a way unlikely ever to be undone. The effect of this separation on their educational opportunities was well stated by a finding in the Kansas case by a court which nevertheless felt compelled to rule against the Negro plaintiffs:

> "Segregation of white and colored children in public schools has a detrimental effect upon the colored children. The impact is greater when it has the sanction of the law; for the policy of separating the races is usually interpreted as denoting the inferiority of the Negro group. A sense of inferiority affects the motivation of a child to learn. Segregation with the sanction of law, therefore, has a tendency to [retard] the educational and mental development of Negro children and to deprive them of some of the benefits they would receive in a racial(ly) integrated school system."[10]

Whatever may have been the extent of psychological knowledge at the time of Plessy v. Ferguson, this finding is amply supported by modern authority.[11] Any language [347 U.S. 483, 495] in Plessy v. Ferguson contrary to this finding is rejected.

We conclude that in the field of public education the doctrine of "separate but equal" has no place. Separate educational facilities are inherently unequal. Therefore, we hold that the plaintiffs and others

similarly situated for whom the actions have been brought are, by rea-
son of the segregation complained of, deprived of the equal protection
of the laws guaranteed by the Fourteenth Amendment. This disposi-
tion makes unnecessary any discussion whether such segregation also
violates the Due Process Clause of the Fourteenth Amendment.[12]

Because these are class actions, because of the wide applicability of
this decision, and because of the great variety of local conditions, the
formulation of decrees in these cases presents problems of considerable
complexity. On reargument, the consideration of appropriate relief
was necessarily subordinated to the primary question—the constitu-
tionality of segregation in public education. We have now announced
that such segregation is a denial of the equal protection of the laws. In
order that we may have the full assistance of the parties in formulat-
ing decrees, the cases will be restored to the docket, and the parties
are requested to present further argument on Questions 4 and 5 previ-
ously propounded by the Court for the reargument this Term.[13] The
Attorney General [347 U.S. 483, 496] of the United States is again
invited to participate. The Attorneys General of the states requiring
or permitting segregation in public education will also be permitted to
appear as amici curiae upon request to do so by September 15, 1954,
and submission of briefs by October 1, 1954.[14]

It is so ordered.

FOOTNOTES

[Footnote 1] In the Kansas case, Brown v. Board of Education, the
plaintiffs are Negro children of elementary school age residing in To-
peka. They brought this action in the United States District Court for
the District of Kansas to enjoin enforcement of a Kansas statute which
permits, but does not require cities of more than 15,000 population to
maintain separate school facilities for Negro and white students. Kan.
Gen. Stat. 72-1724 (1949). Pursuant to that authority, the Topeka
Board of Education elected to establish segregated elementary schools.
Other public schools in the community, however, are operated on a
nonsegregated basis. The three-judge District Court, convened under
28 U.S.C. 2281 and 2284, found that segregation in public education
has a detrimental effect upon Negro children, but denied relief on the

ground that the Negro and white schools were substantially equal with respect to buildings, transportation, curricula, and educational qualifications of teachers. 98 F. Supp. 797. The case is here on direct appeal under 28 U.S.C. 1253. In the South Carolina case, Briggs v. Elliott, the plaintiffs are Negro children of both elementary and high school age residing in Clarendon County. They brought this action in the United States District Court for the Eastern District of South Carolina to enjoin enforcement of provisions in the state constitution and statutory code which require the segregation of Negroes and whites in public schools. S. C. Const., Art. XI, 7; S. C. Code 5377 (1942). The three-judge District Court, convened under 28 U.S.C. 2281 and 2284, denied the requested relief. The court found that the Negro schools were inferior to the white schools and ordered the defendants to begin immediately to equalize the facilities. But the court sustained the validity of the contested provisions and denied the plaintiffs admission [347 U.S. 483, 487] to the white schools during the equalization program. 98 F. Supp. 529. This Court vacated the District Court's judgment and remanded the case for the purpose of obtaining the court's views on a report filed by the defendants concerning the progress made in the equalization program. 342 U.S. 350. On remand, the District Court found that substantial equality had been achieved except for buildings and that the defendants were proceeding to rectify this inequality as well. 103 F. Supp. 920. The case is again here on direct appeal under 28 U.S.C. 1253. In the Virginia case, Davis v. County School Board, the plaintiffs are Negro children of high school age residing in Prince Edward county. They brought this action in the United States District Court for the Eastern District of Virginia to enjoin enforcement of provisions in the state constitution and statutory code which require the segregation of Negroes and whites in public schools. Va. Const., 140; Va. Code 22–221 (1950). The three-judge District Court, convened under 28 U.S.C. 2281 and 2284, denied the requested relief. The court found the Negro school inferior in physical plant, curricula, and transportation, and ordered the defendants forthwith to provide substantially equal curricula and transportation and to "proceed with all reasonable diligence and dispatch to remove" the inequality in physical plant. But, as in the South Carolina case, the court sustained the validity of the contested provisions and denied the plaintiffs admis-

sion to the white schools during the equalization program. 103 F. Supp. 337. The case is here on direct appeal under 28 U.S.C. 1253. In the Delaware case, Gebhart v. Belton, the plaintiffs are Negro children of both elementary and high school age residing in New Castle County. They brought this action in the Delaware Court of Chancery to enjoin enforcement of provisions in the state constitution and statutory code which require the segregation of Negroes and whites in public schools. Del. Const., Art. X, 2; Del. Rev. Code 2631 (1935). The Chancellor gave judgment for the plaintiffs and ordered their immediate admission to schools previously attended only by white children, on the ground that the Negro schools were inferior with respect to teacher training, pupil-teacher ratio, extracurricular activities, physical plant, and time and distance involved [347 U.S. 483, 488] in travel. 87 A. 2d 862. The Chancellor also found that segregation itself results in an inferior education for Negro children (see note 10, infra), but did not rest his decision on that ground. Id., at 865. The Chancellor's decree was affirmed by the Supreme Court of Delaware, which intimated, however, that the defendants might be able to obtain a modification of the decree after equalization of the Negro and white schools had been accomplished. 91 A. 2d 137, 152. The defendants, contending only that the Delaware courts had erred in ordering the immediate admission of the Negro plaintiffs to the white schools, applied to this Court for certiorari. The writ was granted, 344 U.S. 891. The plaintiffs, who were successful below, did not submit a cross-petition.

[Footnote 2] 344 U.S. 1, 141, 891.

[Footnote 3] 345 U.S. 972. The Attorney General of the United States participated both Terms as amicus curiae.

[Footnote 4] For a general study of the development of public education prior to the Amendment, see Butts and Cremin, A History of Education in American Culture (1953), Pts. I, II; Cubberley, Public Education in the United States (1934 ed.), cc. II–XII. School practices current at the time of the adoption of the Fourteenth Amendment are described in Butts and Cremin, supra, at 269–275; Cubberley, supra, at 288–339, 408–431; Knight, Public Education in the South (1922), cc. VIII, IX. See also H. Ex. Doc. No. 315, 41st Cong., 2d Sess. (1871). Although the demand for free public schools followed substantially the same pattern in both the North and the South, the development

in the South did not begin to gain momentum until about 1850, some twenty years after that in the North. The reasons for the somewhat slower development in the South (e.g., the rural character of the South and the different regional attitudes toward state assistance) are well explained in Cubberley, supra, at 408–423. In the country as a whole, but particularly in the South, the War [347 U.S. 483, 490] virtually stopped all progress in public education. Id., at 427–428. The low status of Negro education in all sections of the country, both before and immediately after the War, is described in Beale, A History of Freedom of Teaching in American Schools (1941), 112–132, 175–195. Compulsory school attendance laws were not generally adopted until after the ratification of the Fourteenth Amendment, and it was not until 1918 that such laws were in force in all the states. Cubberley, supra, at 563–565.

[Footnote 5] Slaughter-House Cases, 16 Wall. 36, 67–72 (1873); Strauder v. West Virginia, 100 U.S. 303, 307–308 (1880): "It ordains that no State shall deprive any person of life, liberty, or property, without due process of law, or deny to any person within its jurisdiction the equal protection of the laws. What is this but [347 U.S. 483, 491] declaring that the law in the States shall be the same for the black as for the white; that all persons, whether colored or white, shall stand equal before the laws of the States, and, in regard to the colored race, for whose protection the amendment was primarily designed, that no discrimination shall be made against them by law because of their color? The words of the amendment, it is true, are prohibitory, but they contain a necessary implication of a positive immunity, or right, most valuable to the colored race,—the right to exemption from unfriendly legislation against them distinctively as colored,—exemption from legal discriminations, implying inferiority in civil society, lessening the security of their enjoyment of the rights which others enjoy, and discriminations which are steps towards reducing them to the condition of a subject race." See also Virginia v. Rives, 100 U.S. 313, 318 (1880); Ex parte Virginia, 100 U.S. 339, 344–345 (1880).

[Footnote 6] The doctrine apparently originated in Roberts v. City of Boston, 59 Mass. 198, 206 (1850), upholding school segregation against attack as being violative of a state constitutional guarantee of equality. Segregation in Boston public schools was eliminated in 1855.

Mass. Acts 1855, c. 256. But elsewhere in the North segregation in public education has persisted in some communities until recent years. It is apparent that such segregation has long been a nationwide problem, not merely one of sectional concern.

[Footnote 7] See also Berea College v. Kentucky, 211 U.S. 45 (1908).

[Footnote 8] In the Cumming case, Negro taxpayers sought an injunction requiring the defendant school board to discontinue the operation of a high school for white children until the board resumed operation of a high school for Negro children. Similarly, in the Gong Lum case, the plaintiff, a child of Chinese descent, contended only that state authorities had misapplied the doctrine by classifying him with Negro children and requiring him to attend a Negro school.

[Footnote 9] In the Kansas case, the court below found substantial equality as to all such factors. 98 F. Supp. 797, 798. In the South Carolina case, the court below found that the defendants were proceeding "promptly and in good faith to comply with the court's decree." 103 F. Supp. 920, 921. In the Virginia case, the court below noted that the equalization program was already "afoot and progressing" (103 F. Supp. 337, 341); since then, we have been advised, in the Virginia Attorney General's brief on reargument, that the program has now been completed. In the Delaware case, the court below similarly noted that the state's equalization program was well under way. 91 A. 2d 137, 149.

[Footnote 10] A similar finding was made in the Delaware case: "I conclude from the testimony that in our Delaware society, State-imposed segregation in education itself results in the Negro children, as a class, receiving educational opportunities which are substantially inferior to those available to white children otherwise similarly situated." 87 A. 2d 862, 865.

[Footnote 11] K. B. Clark, Effect of Prejudice and Discrimination on Personality Development (Midcentury White House Conference on Children and Youth, 1950); Witmer and Kotinsky, Personality in the Making (1952), c. VI; Deutscher and Chein, The Psychological Effects of Enforced Segregation: A Survey of Social Science Opinion, 26 J. Psychol. 259 (1948); Chein, What are the Psychological Effects of [347 U.S. 483, 495] Segregation Under Conditions of Equal Facilities?, 3 Int. J. Opinion and Attitude Res. 229 (1949); Brameld, Educational Costs, in Discrimination and National Welfare (MacIver, ed., (1949),

44–48; Frazier, The Negro in the United States (1949), 674–681. And see generally Myrdal, An American Dilemma (1944).

[Footnote 12] See Bolling v. Sharpe, post, p. 497, concerning the Due Process Clause of the Fifth Amendment.

[Footnote 13] "4. Assuming it is decided that segregation in public schools violates the Fourteenth Amendment "(a) would a decree necessarily follow providing that, within the [347 U.S. 483, 496] limits set by normal geographic school districting, Negro children should forthwith be admitted to schools of their choice, or "(b) may this Court, in the exercise of its equity powers, permit an effective gradual adjustment to be brought about from existing segregated systems to a system not based on color distinctions? "5. On the assumption on which questions 4 (a) and (b) are based, and assuming further that this Court will exercise its equity powers to the end described in question 4 (b), "(a) should this Court formulate detailed decrees in these cases; "(b) if so, what specific issues should the decrees reach; "(c) should this Court appoint a special master to hear evidence with a view to recommending specific terms for such decrees; "(d) should this Court remand to the courts of first instance with directions to frame decrees in these cases, and if so what general directions should the decrees of this Court include and what procedures should the courts of first instance follow in arriving at the specific terms of more detailed decrees?"

[Footnote 14] See Rule 42, Revised Rules of this Court (effective July 1, 1954). [347 U.S. 483, 497]

List of Cases for which Associate Justice Marshall Was the Majority Author

Supreme Court case	Docket number	Court hearing dates	Supreme Court vote
Mempa v. Rhay	16	10/11/1967–11/13/1967	9–0
Case-Swayne Co. v. Sunkist Growers	66	10/18/1967–12/18/1967	8–1
Powell v. Texas	405	03/07/1968–06/17/1968	5–4
American Lines v. L.&N.R. Co.	797	04/23/1968–06/17/1968	8–1
Pickering v. Board of Education	510	03/27/1968–06/03/1968	8–1
Sabbath v. United States	898	05/02/1968–06/03/1968	8–1
Food Employees v. Logan Plaza	478	03/14/1968–05/20/1968	6–3
First Nat. Bank v. Cities Service	23	11/09/1967–05/20/1968	5–3
Barber v. Page	703	03/28/1968–04/23/1968	9–0
Interstate Circuit v. Dallas	56	01/15/1968–04/22/1968	8–1
Evans v. Cornman	236	01/22/1970–06/15/1970	8–0
NLRB v. Raytheon Co.	440	02/26/1970–05/18/1970	8–0
Choctaw Nation v. Oklahoma	41	10/22/1969–04/27/1970	4–3
Woodward v. Commissioner	412	02/26/1970–04/20/1970	8–0
United States v. Hilton Hotels	528	02/26/1970–04/20/1970	8–0
United States v. Key	402	01/21/1970–03/30/1970	8–0
United States v. Estate of Donnelly	104	01/12/1970–03/23/1970	5–3
United States v. Davis	282	01/12/1970–03/23/1970	5–3

(*Continued*)

List of Cases for which Associate Justice Marshall Was the Majority Author (Continued)

Supreme Court case	Docket number	Court hearing dates	Supreme Court vote
Goldstein v. Cox	66	11/17/1969–01/26/1970	6–2
NLRB v. Rutter-Rex Mfg. Co.	32	10/22/1969–12/15/1969	5–0
Grayned v. City of Rockford	70-5106	01/19/1972–06/26/1972	9–0
Police Dept. of Chicago v. Mosley	70-87	01/19/1972–06/26/1972	9–0
Peters v. Kliff	71-5078	02/22/1972–06/22/1972	6–3
Mcneil v. Director, Patuxent Institution	71-5144	04/20/1972–06/19/1972	9–0
Brunette Machine Wks. v. Kockum Industries	70-314	03/23/1972–06/07/1972	9–0
Caplin v. Marine Midland Grace Trust Co.	70-220	03/28/1972–05/22/1972	5–4
United States v. Topco Associates	70-82	11/16/1971–03/29/1972	6–1
Humphrey v. Cady	70-5004	12/07/1971–03/22/1972	7–0
Dunn v. Blumstein	70-13	11/16/1971–03/21/1972	6–1
United States v. Mississippi Chemical Corp	70-52	01/10/1972–03/06/1972	8–0
Hawaii v. Standard Oil Co.	70-49	10/21/1971–03/01/1972	5–2
Trbovich v. Mine Workers	71-119	11/18/1971–01/17/1972	6–1
SEC v. Medical Committee For Human Rights	70-61	11/10/1971–01/10/1972	6–1
United States v. Bass	70-71	10/18/1971–12/20/1971	5–2
Britt v. North Carolina	70-5041	10/14/1971–12/13/1971	5–2
Atchison, T. & S. F. R. Co. v. Wichita Bd. of Trade	72-214	02/28/1973–06/18/1973	5–3

List of Cases for which Associate Justice Marshall Was the Majority Author (*Continued*)

Supreme Court case	Docket number	Court hearing dates	Supreme Court vote
Wardius v. Oregon	71-6042	01/10/1973– 06/11/1973	9–0
United States v. Mason	72-654	04/18/1973– 06/04/1973	9–0
United States v. Mississippi Tax Comm'n	72-350	03/19/1973– 06/04/1973	7–2
Moor v. County of Alameda	72-10	02/27/1973– 05/14/1973	8–1
Fmc v. Seatrain Lines, Inc.	71-1647	03/21/1973– 05/14/1973	9–0
Linda R. S. v. Richard D.	71-6078	12/06/1972– 03/05/1973	7–2
Bradley v. United States	71-1304	01/08/1973– 03/05/1973	8–1
Heublein, Inc. v. South Carolina Tax Comm'n	71-879	11/13/1972– 12/18/1972	8–0
Erlenbaugh v. United States	71-839	11/13/1972– 12/12/1972	8–0
Tidewater Oil Co. v. United States	71-366	10/11/1072– 12/06/1972	6–3
Letter Carriers v. Austin	72-1180	11/14/1973– 06/25/1974	6–3
Howard Johnson Co. v. Hotel Employees	73-631	03/19/1974– 06/03/1974	8–1
Coming Glass Works v. Brennan	73-29	03/25/1974– 06/03/1974	5–3
Anderson v. United States	73-346	03/19/1974– 06/03/1974	7–2
Bellis v. United States	73-190	02/25/1974– 05/28/1974	8–1
F. D. Rich Co. v. Industrial Lumber Co.	72-1382	01/09/1974– 05/28/1974	8–1
Cooper Stevedoring Co. v. Kopke, Inc.	73-726	04/15/1974– 05/28/1974	8–0

(*Continued*)

List of Cases for which Associate Justice Marshall Was the Majority Author (*Continued*)

Supreme Court case	Docket number	Court hearing dates	Supreme Court vote
Pernell v. Southall Realty	72-6041	02/19/1974– 04/24/1974	9–0
Granny Goose Foods, Inc. v. Teamsters	72-1566	01/08/1974– 03/04/1974	9–0
Memorial Hospital v. Maricopa County	72-847	11/06/1973– 02/26/1974	8–1
Curtis v. Loether	72-1035	12/04/1973– 02/20/1974	9–0
Bonelli Cattle Co. v. Arizona	72-397	10/15/1973– 12/17/1973	7–1
Espinoza v. Farah Mfg. Co.	72-671	10/10/1973– 11/19/1973	8–1
Laing v. United States	73-1808	01/21/1975– 01/13/1976	5–3
United States v. Hale	74-364	04/14/1975– 06/23/1975	9–0
Murphy v. Florida	74-5116	04/15/1975– 06/16/1975	8–1
Fry v. United States	73-822	11/11/1974– 05/27/1974	7–1
Securities Investor Protection v. Barbour	73-2055	03/17/1975– 05/19/1975	8–1
Hill v. Stone	73-1723	01/14/1975– 05/12/1975	5–3
Austin v. New Hampshire	73-2060	01/15/1975– 03/19/1975	7–1
United States v. Wilson	73-1395	12/09/1974– 02/25/1975	7–2
Foster v. Dravo Corp	73-1773	01/20/1975– 02/18/1975	8–0
Harris County Comm'rs Court v. Moore	73-1475	11/11/1974– 02/18/1975	8–1
Emporium Capwell Co. v. Community Org.	73-696	10/22/1974– 02/18/1975	8–1
Usery v. Turner Elkhorn Mining Co.	74-1302	12/02/1975– 07/01/1976	6–2

List of Cases for which Associate Justice Marshall Was the Majority Author (*Continued*)

Supreme Court case	Docket number	Court hearing dates	Supreme Court vote
Union Electric Co. v. EPA	74-1542	01/21/1976– 06/25/1976	9–0
McDonald v. Santa Fe Trail Transp. Co.	75-260	04/20/1976– 06/25/1976	9–0
Fea v. Algonquin SNG, Inc.	75-382	04/20/1976– 06/17/1976	9–0
Kleppe v. New Mexico	74-1488	03/23/1976– 06/17/1976	9–0
Oil Workers v. Mobil Oil Corp.	74-1254	3/29/1976– 06/14/1976	7–2
Kerr v. United States District Court	74-1023	11/11/1975– 06/14/1976	8–0
Tsc Industries, Inc. v. Northway, Inc.	74-1471	03/03/1976– 06/14/1976	8–0
Tennessee v. Dunlap	75-95	03/22/1976– 06/10/1976	9–0
City of Charlotte v. Firefighters	75-250	03/03/1976– 06/07/1976	9–0
Train v. Colorado Pub. Int. Research Group	74-1270	12/09/1975– 06/01/1976	8–0
Hospital Bldg. Co. v. Rex Hospital Trustees	74-1452	02/25/1976– 05/24/1976	9–0
Dann v. Johnston	74-1033	12/09/1975– 03/31/1976	7–0
United States v. United Continental Tuna	74-869	11/03/1975– 03/30/1976	7–1
American Foreign S. S. Co. v. Matise	74-966	10/14/1975– 12/16/1975	8–0
Zenith Radio Corp. v. United States	77-539	04/25/1978– 06/21/1978	9–0
Sanabria v. United States	76-1040	11/08/1977– 06/14/1978	7–2
Agosto v. Ins	76-1410	02/28/1978– 06/06/1978	7–2

(*Continued*)

List of Cases for which Associate Justice Marshall Was the Majority Author (*Continued*)

Supreme Court case	Docket number	Court hearing dates	Supreme Court vote
Robertson v. Wegmann	77-178	03/21/1978– 05/31/1978	6–3
Andrus v. Charlestone Stone Products Co.	77-380	04/18/1978– 05/31/1978	9–0
United States v. Sotelo	76-1800	02/22/1978– 05/22/1978	5–4
Kulko v. California Superior Court	77-293	03/29/1978– 05/15/1978	6–3
Santa Clara Pueblo v. Martinez	76-682	11/29/1977– 05/15/1978	7–1
United States v. Culbert	77-142	01/11/1978– 03/28/1978	8–0
Lorillard v. Pons	76-1346	12/06/1977– 02/22/1978	8–0
J.W. Bateson Co. v. Board of Trustees	76-1476	11/30/1977– 02/22/1978	6–2
Quilloin v. Walcott	76-6372	11/09/1977– 01/10/1978	9–0
United States v. Rutherford	78-605	04/25/1979– 06/18/1979	
United Gas Pipe Line Co. v. McCombs	78-17	02/22/1979– 06/18/1979	8–0
Dunn v. United States	77-6949	03/28/1979– 06/04/1979	8–0
United States v. Batchelder	78-776	04/18/1979– 06/04/1979	9–0
Electrical Workers v. Foust	78-38	02/26/1979– 05/29/1979	9–0
Alexander v. U.S. Dept. of HUD	77-874	12/05/1978– 04/17/1979	9–0
United States v. Kimbell Foods, Inc.	77-1359	01/08/1979– 04/02/1979	9–0
Miller v. Youakim	77-742	10/30/1978– 02/22/1979	8–0
Illinois Elections Bd. v. Socialist Workers Party	77-1248	11/06/1978– 02/22/1979	9–0

List of Cases for which Associate Justice Marshall Was the Majority Author (*Continued*)

Supreme Court case	Docket number	Court hearing dates	Supreme Court vote
Montana v. United States	77-1134	12/04/1978–02/22/1979	8–1
Board of Governors v. First Lincolnwood Corp.	77-832	10/11/1978–12/11/1978	7–2
Dougherty County Board of Education v. White	77-120	10/02/1978–11/28/1978	5–4
White Mountain Apache Tribe v. Bracker	78-1177	01/14/1980–06/27/1980	6–3
Central Machinery Co. v. Arizona Tax Comm'n	78-1604	01/14/1980–06/27/1980	5–4
Exxon Corp. v. Wisconsin Dept. of Revenue	79-509	03/18/1980–06/10/1980	5–4
Coffy v. Republic Steel Corp.	79-81	02/27/1980–06/10/1980	9–0
Walker v. Armco Steel Corp.	78-1862	01/08/1980–06/02/1980	9–0
Gomez v. Toledo	79-5601	04/16/1980–05/27/1980	9–0
Marshall v. Jerrico, Inc.	79-253	03/19/1980–04/28/1980	9–0
City of Rome v. United States	78-1840	10/10/1979–04/22/1980	6–3
United States v. Mitchell	78-1756	12/03/1979–04/15/1980	5–3
Bloomer v. Liberty Mutual Ins. Co.	78-1418	12/04/1979–03/03/1980	8–1
United States v. Clark	78-1513	10/31/1979–02/26/1980	7–2
Rush v. Savchuk	78-952	10/03/1979–01/21/1980	7–2
Merrion v. Jicarilla Apache Tribe	80-11	03/30/1981–01/25/1982	6–3
Arkansas Louisiana Gas Co. v. Hall	78-1789	04/20/1981–07/07/1981	5–3

(*Continued*)

List of Cases for which Associate Justice Marshall Was the Majority Author (*Continued*)

Supreme Court case	Docket number	Court hearing dates	Supreme Court vote
Commonwealth Edison Co. v. Montana	80-581	03/30/1981– 07/02/1981	6–3
California Medical Assn. v. Fec	79-1952	01/19/1981– 06/26/1981	5–0
Donovan v. Dewey	80-901	04/28/1981– 06/17/1981	8–1
Hodel v. Indiana	80-231	02/23/1981– 06/15/1981	9–0
Hodel v. Virginia Surface Mining & Recl. Assn.	79-1538	02/23/1981– 06/15/1981	9–0
Alessi v. Raybestos-Manhattan, Inc.	79-1943	03/04/1981– 05/18/1981	8–0
Steagald v. United States	79-6777	01/14/1981– 04/21/1981	7–2
Kirchberg v. Feenstra	79-1388	12/10/1980– 03/23/1981	9–0
Chicago & N. W. Tr. Co. v. Kalo Brick & Tile	79-1336	12/09/1980– 03/09/1981	9–0
Weaver v. Graham	79-5780	11/05/1980– 02/24/1980	9–0
Fedorenko v. United States	79-5602	10/15/1980– 01/21/1981	7–2
Firestone Tire & Rubber Co. v. Risjord	79-1420	11/12/1980– 01/13/1981	9–0
Ramah Navajo School Bd. v. Bureau of Revenue	80-2162	04/28/1982– 07/02/1982	6–3
Loretto v. Teleprompter Manhattan Catv Corp.	81-244	03/30/1982– 06/30/1982	6–3
Foremost Insurance Co. v. Richardson	80-2134	01/12/1982– 06/23/1982	5–4
Taylor v. Alabama	81-5152	03/23/1982– 06/23/1982	5–4
Patsy v. Florida Board of Regents	80-1874	03/02/1982– 06/21/1982	7–2

List of Cases for which Associate Justice Marshall Was the Majority Author (*Continued*)

Supreme Court case	Docket number	Court hearing dates	Supreme Court vote
Steelworkers v. Sadlowski	81-395	03/31/1982–06/14/1982	5–4
Blum v. Bacon	81-770	04/28/1982–06/14/1982	9–0
Summit Valley Industries, Inc. v. Carpenters	81-497	04/28/1982–06/01/1982	9–0
Woelke & Romero Framing, Inc. v. NLRB	80-1798	03/03/1982–05/24/1982	9–0
Underwriters Assur. Co. v. N.C. Guaranty assn.	80-1496	11/09/1981–03/24/1982	9–0
Hoffman Estates v. Flipside, Hoffman Estates	80-1681	12/09/1981–03/02/1982	8–0
Ralston v. Robinson	80-2049	10/05/1981–12/02/1981	6–3
Piper Aircraft Co. v. Reyno	80-848	10/14/1981–12/08/1981	4–3
United States v. Mitchell	81-1748	03/01/1983–06/27/1983	6–3
Bolger v. Youngs Drug Products Corp.	81-1590	01/12/1983–06/24/1983	8–0
Mennonite Board of Missions v. Adams	82-11	03/30/1983–06/22/1983	6–3
Haring v. Prosise	81-2169	04/20/1983–06/13/1983	9–0
Exxon Corp. v. Eagerton	81-1020	02/22/1983–06/08/1983	9–0
Watt v. Western Nuclear, Inc.	81-1686	01/17/1983–06/06/1983	5–4
General Motors Corp. v. Devex Corp.	81-1661	12/07/1982–05/24/1983	9–0
Pallas Shipping Agency, Ltd. v. Duris	82-502	04/25/1983–05/23/1983	9–0
American Paper Inst. v. American Elec. Power	82-34	03/22/1983–05/16/1983	8–0

(Continued)

List of Cases for which Associate Justice Marshall Was the Majority Author (Continued)

Supreme Court case	Docket number	Court hearing dates	Supreme Court vote
Tuten v. United States	81-6756	03/01/1983–03/30/1983	9–0
Block v. Neal	81-1494	01/19/1983–03/07/1983	9–0
Memphis Bank & Trust Co. v. Garner	81-1	11/29/1982–01/24/1983	9–0
Herman & Maclean v. Huddleston	81-680	11/09/1982–01/24/1983	8–0
Colorado v. New Mexico	80-ORIG	10/04/1982–12/13/1982	9–0
Brown v. Socialist Workers '74 Campaign Comm.	81-776	10/04/1982–12/08/1982	6–3
Berkemer v. Mccarty	83-710	04/18/1984–07/02/1984	9–0
Burnett v. Grattan	83-264	03/26/1984–06/27/1984	9–0
Washington Metro. Transit Auth. v. Johnson	83-747	04/24/1984–06/26/1984	6–3
SEC v. O'Brien	83-751	04/17/1984–06/18/1984	9–0
Hayfield Northern R. Co. v. Chicago & N. W. Tr. Co.	82-1579	02/21/1984–06/12/1984	9–0
California v. Trombetta	83-305	04/18/1984–06/11/1984	9–0
Icc v. American Trucking Assns., Inc.	82-1643	01/10/1984–06/05/1984	5–4
Bernal v. Fainter	83-630	03/28/1984–05/30/1984	8–1
Kirby Forest Industries, Inc. v. United States	82-1994	02/22/1984–05/21/1984	9–0
EEOC v. Shell Oil Co.	82-825	10/31/1983–04/02/1984	9–0
Kosak v. United States	82-618	11/07/1983–03/21/1984	8–1
Heckler v. Edwards	82-874	11/30/1983–03/21/1984	9–0

List of Cases for which Associate Justice Marshall Was the Majority Author (*Continued*)

Supreme Court case	Docket number	Court hearing dates	Supreme Court vote
Dixson v. United States	82-5279	10/12/1983–02/22/1984	5–4
Solem v. Bartlett	82-1253	12/07/1983–02/22/1984	9–0
Aloha Airlines, Inc. v. Director of Taxation	82-585	10/04/1983–11/01/1983	9–0
Kentucky v. Graham	84-849	04/16/1985–06/28/1985	9–0
Central States, Southeast and Southwest Pension Fund v. Central Transport, Inc.	82-2157	11/27/1984–06/19/1985	9–0
Johnson v. Mayor & City Council of Baltimore	84-518	04/22/1985–06/17/1985	9–0
Caldwell v. Mississippi	83-6607	02/25/2985–06/11/1985	5–3
Hillsborough County v. Automated Medical Labs	83-1925	04/16/1985–06/03/1985	9–0
United States v. Locke	83-1394	11/06/1984–04/01/1985	6–3
United States v. Miller	83-1750	01/16/1985–04/01/1985	8–0
National R. Passenger Corp. v. A.T. & S. F. Co.	83-1492	01/15/1985–03/18/1985	8–0
Dean Witter Reynolds Ins. v. Byrd	83-1708	12/04/1884–03/04/1985	9–0
Ake v. Oklahoma	83-5424	11/07/1984–02/20/1985	8–1
Alexander v. Choate	83-727	10/01/1984–01/09/1985	9–0
Tiffany Fine Arts, Inc. v. United States	83-1007	10/31/1984–01/09/1985	9–0
Tashjian v. Republican Party of Connecticut	85-766	10/08/1986–12/10/1986	5–4
California Federal S & L Assn. v. Guerra	85-494	10/08/1986–01/13/1987	6–3

(*Continued*)

List of Cases for which Associate Justice Marshall Was the Majority Author (*Continued*)

Supreme Court case	Docket number	Court hearing dates	Supreme Court vote
West Virginia v. United States	85-937	11/10/1986– 01/10/1986	9–0
Rankin v. McPherson	85-2068	03/23/1987– 06/24/1987	5–4
Puerto Rico v. Branstad	85-2116	03/30/1987– 06/23/1987	9–0
Perry v. Thomas	86-566	04/28/1987– 06/15/1987	7–2
Rose v. Rose	85-1206	03/04/1987– 05/18/1987	8–1
Burlington No. R. Co. v. Okla. Tax Comm'n	86-337	03/25/1987– 04/28/1987	9–0
United States v. General Dynamics Corp.	85-1385	01/13/1987– 04/22/1987	6–3
Brock v. Roadway Express, Inc.	85-1530	12/03/1986– 04/22/1987	6–3
Arkansas Writers' Project, Inc. v. Ragland	85-1370	01/20/1987– 04/22/1987	7–2
FCC v. Florida Power Corp.	85-1658	12/03/1986– 02/25/1987	9–0
Burlington Northern R. Co. v. Woods	85-1088	11/04/1986– 02/24/1987	9–0
Iowa Mutual Ins. Co. v. Laplante	85-1589	12/01/1986– 02/24/1987	8–1
Gwaltney v. Chesapeake Bay Foundation	86-473	10/05/1987– 12/01/1987	8–0
Westfall v. Erwin	86-714	11/02/1987– 01/13/1988	8–0
Thompson v. Thompson	86-964	10/06/1987– 01/12/1988	8–0
Carnegie-Mellon Univ. v. Cohill	86-1021	11/10/1987– 01/20/1988	5–3
Torres v. Oakland Scavenger Co.	86-1845	02/23/1988– 06/24/1988	8–1

List of Cases for which Associate Justice Marshall Was the Majority Author (Continued)

Supreme Court case	Docket number	Court hearing dates	Supreme Court vote
Department of Justice v. Tax Analysis	88-782	04/24/1989–06/23/1989	8–1
Newman-Green, Inc. v. Alfonzo Larrain	88-774	04/24/1989–06/12/1989	7–2
Mead Corp. v. Tilley	87-1868	02/22/1989–06/05/1989	8–1
Hernandez v. Commissioner	87-963	11/28/1988–06/05/1989	5–2
Community For Creative Non Violence v. Reid	88-293	03/29/1989–06/05/1989	9–0
Mansell v. Mansell	87-201	01/10/1989–05/30/1989	7–2
Neitzke v. Williams	87-1882	02/22/1989–05/01/1989	9–0
Blanton v. North Las Vegas	87-1437	01/09/1989–03/06/1989	9–0
Eu v. San Francisco Democratic Comm.	87-1269	12/05/1988–02/22/1989	8–0
Sheet Metal Workers v. Lynn	86-1940	11/07/1988–01/18/1989	8–0
Goldberg v. Sweet	87-826	10/12/1988–01/10/1989	9–0
Owens v. Okure	87-56	11/01/1988–01/10/1989	9–0
Sisson v. Ruby	88-2041	04/23/1990–06/25/1990	9–0
Pennsylvania Public Welfare Dept. v. Davenport	89-156	02/20/1990–05/29/1990	7–2
Hughey v. United States	89-5691	03/27/1990–05/21/1990	9–0
United States v. Munoz-Flores	88-1685	02/20/1990–05/21/1990	9–0
NLRB v. Curtin Matheson Scientific, Inc.	88-1685	12/04/1989–04/17/1990	5–4

(Continued)

List of Cases for which Associate Justice Marshall Was the Majority Author (*Continued*)

Supreme Court case	Docket number	Court hearing dates	Supreme Court vote
Austin v. Michigan Chamber of Commerce	88-1569	10/31/1989– 03/27/1990	6–3
Lytle v. Household Mfg., Inc.	88-334	01/08/1990– 03/20/1990	9–0
Teamster v. Terry	88-1719	12/06/1989– 03/20/1990	6–3
Mckoy v. North Carolina	88-5909	10/10/1989– 03/05/1990	6–3
Reves v. Ernst & Young	88-1480	11/27/1989– 02/21/1990	5–4
United States v. Goodyear Tire & Rubber Co.	88-1474	11/01/1989– 12/11/1989	9–0
Northbrook National Ins. Co. v. Brewer	89-7260	10/04/1989– 11/07/1989	8–1
Burns v. United States	89-7260	12/03/1990– 06/13/1991	5–4
Johnson v. Home State Bank	90-693	04/16/1991– 06/10/1991	9–0
Exxon Corp. v. Central Gulf Lines Inc.	90-34	04/15/1991– 06/03/1991	9–0
Primate Protection League v. Tulane Education Fund.	90-89	03/20/1991– 05/20/1991	8–0
Cottage Savings Assoc. v. Commissioner of Internal Revenue	89-1965	01/15/1991– 04/07/1991	7–2
United States v. Centennial Savings Bank	89-1926	01/15.1991– 04/17/1991	7–2
Eastern Airlines, Inc. v. Floyd	89-1598	10/29/1990– 04/17/1991	9–0
Martin v. Oshre	89-1541	11/27/1990– 03/20/1991	9–0
United States v. Smith	89-1646	11/07/1990– 03/20/1991	8–1
Firstier Mtge. Co. v. Investors Mtge. Ins. Co.	89-1063	10/10/1990– 01/15/1991	9–0
Moskal v. United States	89-964	10/01/1990– 12/03/1990	5–3

BIBLIOGRAPHY

Alfred, Lisa. *Thurgood Marshall*. New York: Chelsea House Publishers, 2005.

The American Presidency Project. *Lyndon B. Johnson: Remarks at the Swearing in of Judge Thurgood Marshall as Solicitor General, August 24, 1965*. University of California, Santa Barbara, 2011. http://www.presidency.ucsb.edu.

Armstead, Ron E. "Veterans in the Fight for Equal Rights: From the Civil War to Today." *The Trotter Review* 18, no. 1 (2009): 92–105.

Baker, T.H. *Thurgood Marshall Oral History Interview I, 7/10/69*. Austin, TX: Lyndon Baines Johnson Library, 1969.

Ball, Howard. *A Defiant Life: Thurgood Marshall and the Persistence of Racism in America*. New York: Random House Publishing, 1998.

Beito, David T., and Beito, Linda Royster. *Black Maverick: T.R.M. Howard's Fight for Civil Rights and Economic Power*. Champaign: University of Illinois Press, 2009.

Bellantoni, Christina. *Thurgood Marshall Takes Center Stage At Kagan Hearings*. New York: Talking Points Memo, June 28, 2010. http://tpmdc.talkingpointsmemo.com.

Bragg, Christine. *Vietnam, Korea and U.S. Foreign Policy, 1945–1975.* Oxford: Educational Heinemann Publishing Company, 2005.

Branch, Taylor. *At Canaan's Edge: America in the King Years 1965–1968.* New York: Simon & Schuster, 2006.

Brown-Nagin, Tomiko. *Courage to Dissent: Atlanta and the Long History of the Civil Rights Movement.* New York: Oxford University Press, 2011.

Bureau of International Information Program. *Free at Last: The U.S. Civil Rights Movement.* Washington, D.C.: U.S. Department of State, 2008.

Bush, George H. W. *Letter on the Resignation of United States Supreme Court Associate Justice Thurgood Marshall.* George Bush Presidential Library and Museum, 1991. http://bushlibrary.tamu.edu/research/public_papers.php?id=3147&year=1991&month=6.

Carter, Liz, and Yackley, Deborah A. "Civil Rights Giant and First Black Supreme Court Justice Thurgood Marshall Honored on Black Heritage Stamp Series." *Postal News.* Washington, D.C.: United States Postal Service, December 16, 2002.

Coleman, David G., Kent, G., Germany, G., McKee, A., and Selverstone, Marc J. *Presidential Recordings of Lyndon B. Johnson: Digital Edition.* Charlottesville: University of Virginia Press, 2010. http://presidentialrecordings.rotunda.upress.virginia.edu.

Coleman, David G., and Matthews, Keri. *Thurgood Marshall & LBJ: From the Johnson Tapes.* Charlottesville, VA: Presidential recordings at the Miller Center of Public Affairs University of Virginia, 2011. http://whitehousetapes.net.

Crowe, Chris. *Thurgood Marshall Up Close.* New York: Penguin Young Readers, 2008.

Davis, Julie H. *GOP Senators Rip Elena Kagan's Work as Thurgood Marshall's Court Clerk.* New York: Associated Press, July 10, 2010. www.cleveland.com.

Davis, Michael D., and Clark, Hunter R. *Thurgood Marshall Warrior at the Bar: Rebel on the Bench.* New York: Carol Publishing Group, 1992.

Dudziak, Mary L. *Exporting American Dreams: Thurgood Marshall's African Journey.* New York: Oxford University Press, 2008.

Eisenhower, Dwight D. "Mob Rule Cannot Be Allowed to Override the Decisions of Our Courts." Address on Little Rock, Arkansas, September 24, 1957. *History Matters.* http://historymatters.gmu.edu/d/6335/.

Ebony magazine. "The Best I Could With What I Had: The Legacy of Thurgood Marshall." 46, no. 11 (September 1991): 109–25.

Ebony magazine. "The Thurgood Marshall." 45, no. 7 (May 1990): 68.

Espo, David. "Late Justice's Legacy Plays out at Kagan Hearings." *Washington Times,* June 29, 2010. http://www.washingtontimes.com/news/2010/jun/29/late-justices-legacy-plays-out-at-kagan-hearings/print/.

Feldman, Ruth T. *Thurgood Marshall.* Minneapolis, MN: Lerner Publications Company, 2001.

Friedman, Michael J. *Free at Last: The U.S. Civil Rights Movement.* Washington, D.C.: U.S. Department of State, Bureau of International Information Programs, 2008.

Gewirtz, Paul. "Thurgood Marshall." *Faculty Scholarship Series.* Paper 1708. New Haven, CT: Yale Law School, Lillian Goldman Law Library, 1991. http://digitalcommons.law.yale.edu/fss_papers/1708.

Goldman, Roger, and Gallen, David. *Thurgood Marshall: Justice for All.* New York: First Carroll & Graf, 1992.

Hand, John T. "Thurgood Marshall's Dissents in Defense of the Poor." *Pace Law Review* 13, no. 2 (1993), 305–12.

Haugen, Brenda. *Thurgood Marshall: Civil Rights Lawyer and Supreme Court Justice.* Minneapolis, MN: Compass Point Books, 2007.

Horn, Geoffrey M. *Thurgood Marshall.* Milwaukee, WI: World Almanac Library, 2004.

Jones, Thelma. "Mrs. Thurgood Marshall is Active in SW." *The Southwester.* August 2008, p. 11.

Kennedy, John F. "Address to the American People on Civil Rights." From the Oval Office, June 11, 1963. http://www.archive.org/details/jfks19630611.

King, Martin Luther Jr. *Western Union Telefax to the Honorable Thurgood Marshall,* July 13, 1967. http://mlk-kpp01.stanford.edu/index.php/encyclopedia/documentsentry/doc_telegram_from_king_to_thurgood_marshall.

Kutler, Stanley. *It's Still All About Race.* July 4, 2010. http://www.huffingtonpost.

Lacher, Irene. "Laurence Fishburne opens in 'Thurgood' at the Geffen Playhouse." *Los Angeles Times,* July 8, 2010. http://latimesblogs.latimes.com.

Marshall, Thurgood. "The Legal Attack to Secure Civil Rights." Speech presented before the NAACP Wartime Conference, Chicago, Illinois, July 13, 1942.

Marshall, Thurgood. "Reflections on the Bicentennial of the United States Constitution." *Harvard Law Review*, 101 (1987), 1–4.

Marshall, Thurgood. "The Sword and the Robe." Speech presented before the Second Circuit Judicial Conference, May 8, 1981.

Mears, Bill. *Tapes Reveal Thurgood Marshall's Rocky Road to the Supreme Court*. February 24, 2011. http://articles.cnn.com/2011.

Myrdal, Gunnar. *An American Dilemma: The Negro Problem and Modern Democracy*. New York: Harper & Brothers, 1944.

New York Times. "Marshall's Assessments of Nation's Notables." Section 1, January 31, 1993, p. 31.

Pfiffner, James P. *The Modern Presidency*. Boston, MA: Wadsworth, Cengage Learning, 2011

Schlesinger, Arthur M., Jr. *Robert Kennedy and His Times*. New York: First Mariner Books, 1978.

Scott, Bill. *1963 Year in Review—Part I: Events of 1963*. Washington, D.C.: United Press International, Inc., 1963.

Shapiro, Herbert. *White Violence and Black Response: From Reconstruction to Montgomery*. Amherst: The University of Massachusetts Press, 1988.

Smith, J. Clay Jr. *Supreme Justice: Speeches and Writing, Thurgood Marshall*. Philadelphia: University of Pennsylvania Press, 2003.

Smith, Stephen, and Ellis, Kate. *Thurgood Marshall: Before The Court*. St. Paul, MN: American RadioWorks, 2011. http://americanradioworks.publicradio.org/features/marshall/.

Time magazine. "The Congress: Poor John." 85, no. 22 (May 28, 1965).

Time magazine. "The Law: The Tension of Change." 67, no. 12 (September 19, 1955): pp. 23–27.

Time magazine. "The Supreme Court: Negro Justice." 89, no. 25 (June 23, 1967). http://www.time.com/time/magazine/article/0,9171,839512,00.html—ixzz1PuoJTMGr.

Time magazine. "The Supreme Court: The First Negro Justice." 90, no. 10 (September 8, 1967).

Tobias, Ted. *In Tribute: Eulogies of Famous People*. Lanham, MD: Scarecrow Press, 1999.

Toobin, Jeffery. *The Nine: Inside the Secret World of the Supreme Court.* New York: Anchor Books, 2008.

Tushnet, Mark V. *Making Civil Rights Law: Thurgood Marshall and the Supreme Court, 1936–1961.* New York: Oxford University Press, 1994.

Tushnet, Mark V. *Making Constitutional Law: Thurgood Marshall and the Supreme Court, 1961–1991.* New York: Oxford University Press, 1997.

UNESCO. *Four statements on the race question.* Paris, France: United Nations Educational, Scientific and Cultural Organization, 1969.

United States Courts. *Profile of Justice Thurgood Marshall.* Washington, D.C.: Administrative Office of the U.S. Courts, 2011. http:// www.uscourts.gov.

University of Maryland School of Law. *Donald Gaines Murray and the Integration of the University of Maryland School of Law.* Baltimore, MD: Thurgood Marshall Law Library, 2011. http://www.law. umaryland.edu/marshall/specialcollections/murray/.

U.S. Congress. *Congressional Record, 84th Congress, 3d session.* 1956, p. 4515–4516.

U.S. Postal Service. *Civil Rights Giant and First Black Supreme Court Justice Honored On 2003 Black Heritage Series Stamp.* Washington, D.C. 2003. www.usps.com

Weist, Andrew. *The Vietnam War.* New York: Rosen Publishing Group, 2009.

Willbanks, James H. *Vietnam War Almanac.* New York: Facts on File, 2009.

Williams, Juan. *Eyes on the Prize: America's Civil Rights Years, 1954–1965.* New York: Penguin Group, 1987.

Williams, Juan. "Nobody Knows." *Ebony* 45, no. 7 (1990): 69–76.

Williams, Juan. *Thurgood Marshall: American Revolutionary.* New York: Three Rivers Press, 1998.

Woodward, Bob. "The Abortion Papers." *Washington Post,* January 22, 1989.

Woodward, Bob, and Armstrong, Scott. *The Brethren: Inside the Supreme Court.* New York: Simon & Schuster, 1979.

INDEX

About the Authors

GLENN L. STARKS, PhD, holds a doctorate in Public Policy and Administration from Virginia Commonwealth University's L. Douglas Wilder School of Government and Public Affairs. He has 20 years of experience working for the U.S. government and has written extensively on public administration and American politics, including two recent books on the history of the U.S. government.

F. ERIK BROOKS, PhD, is an assistant to the dean of the college of liberal arts and social sciences and associate professor in the Department of Political Science at Georgia Southern University, Statesboro. He holds a doctorate in public policy and administration from Virginia Commonwealth University's L. Douglas Wilder School of Government and Public Affairs. He has written extensively on public administration, American politics, and African American history, including Greenwood's *Historically Black Colleges and Universities*.